Morning Praise
and
Evensong

Morning Praise and Evensong

A Liturgy of the Hours in Musical Setting

Fides Publishers Inc., Notre Dame, Ind.

MORNING PRAISE AND EVENSONG
Edited and arranged by
William G. Storey, D.M.S., Frank C. Quinn, O.P., and David F. Wright, O.P.
The Graduate Program in Liturgical Studies
The University of Notre Dame, Notre Dame, Indiana

©Copyright: 1973, Fides Publishers, Inc.
Notre Dame, Indiana

Nihil obstat: Louis J. Putz, C.S.C.   Imprimatur: Leo A. Pursley, D.D.
University of Notre Dame   Bishop of Ft. Wayne-South Bend

ISBN: 0-8190-0411-1

Acknowledgements:

The Beacon Press: Musical arrangement of *Hosmer*, p. 197.

T. & T. Clark: "That man hath perfect blessedness" from Grieve's *The Scottish Metrical Psalter*, p. 182.

The Grail (England): Psalms 4, 8, 18A, 22, 29, 42, 50, 56, 58, 62, 83, 91, 129, 133, 140, 144, from *The Psalms: A Translation* published by William Collins Sons & Co. Ltd.; and the Canticle of Simeon.

Mrs. Robert E. Jeffries: Musical arrangement of *St. Magnus*, p. 153.

Bro. Ephraim Leaman, O.C.S.O.: "Lord Jesus Christ, abide with us," p. 88.

Oxford University Press: "The glory of these forty days," trans. M.F. Bell, p. 133, from *The English Hymnal*; "The King shall come when morning dawns," p. 124; musical arrangements of: *Kingsfold*, p. 22, from *The English Hymnal*; *King's Weston*, p. 180, from *Enlarged Songs of Praise*; *Spires*, from *The English Hymnal*, pp. 9, 140.

Bro. Paul Quenon, O.C.S.O.: "O splendor of eternal light," p. 25.

James Quinn, S.J.: "Bless'd be the God of Israel," p. 22; "Bless'd be the Lord our God," p. 115; "Day is done, but love unfailing," p. 43; "I call, O Lord, on you," p. 4; "May flights of angels lead you on your way," p. 187; "My soul is like the deer," p. 197; "Sing, all creation, sing to God in gladness!" p. 50; "To God with gladness sing," p. 65; from *New Hymns for All Seasons*, published by Geoffrey Chapman Publishers.

The Search Press, Ltd.: "Hail, Redeemer, King Divine," p. 95.

World Library Publications: "A brightness glows o'er all the land," p. 153; "Holy Spirit, come to us," p. 147; "O Christ, you are the light and day," p. 58; "O Lord of light who made the stars," p. 120; "O Sun of Justice, fill our hearts," p. 140; "On this day, the first of days," p. 14; "Out of the depths I cry, O Lord," p. 105; "Praise to Mary, heaven's gate," p. 159; "Sing my tongue the ageless story," p. 134; "Sing to the Lord a joyful song," p. 110; "The Lord is my true shepherd," p. 27. Tunes for: "Sing to the Lord a joyful song," p. 110; and "The Lord is my true shepherd," p. 27. Musical arrangements for: *Aus Tiefer Not*, p. 105; *Dean, in Kentucky Harmony*, 1816, p. 11; *Gott Sei Dank*, p. 14.

Scripture Readings and Canticles are taken from *The New American Bible*, ©1970, and used with permission of The Confraternity of Christian Doctrine.

The Lord's Prayer, the Benedictus, and the Magnificat, ©1970, and used with permission of the *International Consultation on English Texts*.

Cover Design: Michael Rider   **Photo: Thomas Hampson**

Contents

Foreword

Liturgical background

The Constitution on the Sacred Liturgy of the II Vatican Council (Dec. 4, 1963) is the *magna charta* for the renewal and restoration of the public worship of the Roman Catholic Church. The revised liturgical books of the Roman rite that have been gradually appearing since 1963 are the fruit of the reform initiatives taken by the Council.

After the Roman Missal itself (1970), the most important liturgical book to have been promulgated is the *Liturgy of the Hours,* the new Divine Office commissioned under the authority of chapter four of the CSL. The apostolic constitution (*Laudis Canticum*) of Pope Paul VI which prefaces it leaves no doubt as to the seriousness of the Holy See's intentions in carrying out this part of the conciliar reforms. The "General Instruction" (*Institutio Generalis*) which introduces the Liturgy of the Hours is a profoundly theological and pastoral document before being a rubrical and canonical one. Its mandated principles are, of course, those of the II Vatican Council.

> Christ is always present to his Church, especially in her liturgical celebrations. He is present in the sacrifice of the Mass . . . in the sacraments . . . in his word, since it is he himself who speaks when the holy Scriptures are read in the Church. He is present, lastly, when the Church prays and sings, for he promised: 'Where two or three are gathered together in my name, there am I in the midst of them' (Mt 18:20). (CSL, 7)[1]

These theological truths are a prelude to the demand of the Council for

> . . . Full, conscious and active participation in the liturgical celebrations which is demanded by the very nature of the liturgy. Such a participation by the Christian people . . . is their right and duty by reason of their baptism. (CSL, 14)[2]

---

[1] *The Constitution on the Sacred Liturgy and the Motu Proprio of Pope Paul VI,* (Glen Rock, N.J.: The Paulist Press, 1964), p. 33.
[2] *Op. cit.,* p. 36.

The presence of the High Priest of our redemption calls for "the full, conscious and active" response of all his members, and in the restoration of the liturgy which the Council mandated, it was "this full and active participation by all the people" which was the primary aim. To this end the reformed liturgy was to be "nobly simple, reasonably short, clear, unencumbered by useless repetitions and within the people's powers of comprehension." (CSL, 34)[3] The revision of the liturgical books necessary to the rites was to be carried out in this spirit.

Above all the *Liturgy of the Hours* aims at restoring the public and popular character of the morning and evening services: Lauds and Vespers.

By the venerable tradition of the universal Church, Lauds as morning prayer and Vespers as evening prayer are the two hinges on which the daily Office turns; hence they are to be considered as the chief Hours and are to be celebrated as such. (CSL, 89a)[4]

In the same way the GI promotes a new sense of pastoral responsibility for the restoration and maintenance of the Hours in cathedrals, parishes, seminaries, religious houses and homes.

Pastors of souls should see to it that the faithful are invited and helped by requisite instruction to celebrate the chief hours in common, especially on Sundays and feasts.

Communities of canons, monks, nuns and other religious . . . represent the Church at prayer in a special way.

Sacred ministers and other clerics, not otherwise bound to common celebration, who live together or assemble for any purpose should try to say at least some part of the Liturgy of the Hours in common, particularly Lauds in the morning and Vespers in the evening.

Even religious . . . who are not obliged to celebration in common . . . are strongly recommended

[3] *Op. cit.*, p. 42.
[4] *Op. cit.*, p. 58.

to gather together by themselves or with the people to celebrate this liturgy or part of it.

Wherever groups of the laity are gathered . . . they are encouraged to recite the Church's Office, by celebrating part of the Liturgy of the Hours . . . by public worship and prayer they can have an impact on all men and contribute to the salvation of the whole world.

Finally, it is fitting that the family . . . should not only offer common prayer to God but also say certain parts of the Liturgy of the Hours (GI, 20–27)[5]

The GI proposes the "prayer of the Church" to all Christians, prefers communal celebration over private recitation, and strongly recommends the sung Office as the form which "best accords with the nature of this prayer." (33 & 268)

After many years of labor by the Congregation for Divine Worship and its many collaborators throughout the world, the official Latin edition of the *Liturgy of the Hours* is now complete. Its translation into English, however, will take several years and an eventual musical version even longer. More important, it is not anticipated that the Latin original will be reproduced simply as such, without modification or adaptation, in English.

The new *Liturgy of the Hours* is both a precious gift to be received with gratitude and a puzzling problem to be grappled with as reverently, constructively and practically as possible. Again and again the GI warns us not to consider the Office the preserve of the clergy, religious or other elite groups. "It belongs to the whole Christian community." (270) The warning is well taken, but as it stands, the Book of Hours is an acute embarrassment of riches. It is rather hard to see how any save a few elite communities will be able to actually employ the whole thing in their worship. This multivolume work is too rich, too complicated, too laden with the liturgical treasures of the past. It will also be too expensive for most Christians to buy. It is more like some vast repository

---

[5] All quotations from the *General Instruction on the Liturgy of the Hours* are taken from the translation by Peter Coughlan and Peter Purdue. Collegeville, Minnesota: The Liturgical Press, 1971.

of good things, both new and old, than a useable tool for the restoration of the Office. Its very copiousness militates against its effectiveness. Hopefully it will be considered more a treasure-trove to be mined for its contributions than a book to be copied and imitated slavishly.

As a concrete step toward the actual communal celebration of the two major Hours, *Morning Praise and Evensong* proposes to be:

1. a simplified, uncluttered, rubricated edition of Lauds and Vespers for common use;

2. a musical edition of the chief Hours which will strongly promote the fully sung Office and especially the restoration of a variety of psalmodic styles;

3. an incentive to the regular, fully ritualized celebration of the Hours by the many emerging Christian communities, lay, clerical and religious, which are springing up everywhere and searching for authentic, Catholic prayer forms.

While scrupulously respecting the main thrust of the GI, *Morning Praise and Evensong* intends to take full advantage of those paragraphs which permit or encourage the adaptation of the *Liturgy of the Hours* to the needs of communal and popular worship. It will, therefore, maintain intact the basic structure of the Hours: opening hymn, psalmody, Bible reading and prayers (GI, 33), but it will make the following modifications in the interest of simplicity and emphasis:

1. It employs a one-week psalter containing only the most expressive hymns, psalms and canticles for Lauds and Vespers.

2. It omits the short Responses after the readings. (GI, 49)

3. It promotes the use of the full lectionary at these Hours. (GI, 46, 142)

4. It alters the prayers of intercession, at Evensong especially, in the direction of true litanies in order to further participation and more recollected praying, and introduces variety into the introductory versicles and blessings.

5. It encourages a generous use of the pause for silent meditation recommended after the psalmody

and readings and the regular use of psalm collects. (GI, 48, 201–202)

6. It suggests the restoration of the traditional Service of Light (*Lucernarium*) at the beginning of Vespers and the use of incense during Psalm 141 and the Canticles of Zechariah and Mary. (GI, 39, 261)

7. It urges that the Hours be celebrated with appropriate ritual and ceremony. Like music, posture and gestures (standing, sitting, kneeling, bowing, praying with hands extended, the sign of the cross) and the use of incense, lights and vestments should not be considered as merely decorative or as extrinsic to prayer, but as proper to man's nature, conducive to recollection and as revealing more perfectly and fully the communal character of Christian worship. (GI, 270, chap. 5)

By incorporating the above points the authors hope to underline the categorical principle of the GI: "It is of the utmost importance that Lauds and Vespers be the prayer of the Christian community." (40) The best efforts of many Christians will be needed if this foreward-looking statement is to become a reality. It is our conviction that nothing will help smash the stereotype of the silent, solo Office so much as any significant effort at establishing a fully ritualized, sung Liturgy of the Hours. When the Hours can be seen and experienced as an alternation of song and of silence, of ritual and simplicity, of pattern and spontaneity, they will become once more inescapably corporate and genuinely popular.

How to Arrange This Office

This prayer book has five principal parts which require co-ordination:

1. The *Calendar of Feasts* and the *Table* of movable liturgical days need to be consulted regularly for a timely selection of seasonal and festal offices.

2. The *Psalter*, the largely invariable or common part of the daily Office, contains the hymns, psalms, canticles, litanies, etc., appointed for each day of the week at Lauds and Vespers. During the larger part of the year (the 34 weeks between the Baptism of our Lord and Lent and between Pentecost and

Advent), apart from the longer Bible readings (if used), the Office is sung each day as set forth in the Psalter.

3. The *Proper of the Seasons* contains the special hymns, short lessons, antiphons, litanies, collects and blessings appropriate to Advent, Christmastide, Lent and Eastertide. Whatever is found in this Proper replaces what is ordinarily used in the Psalter. Each new season, like Sundays and solemnities, begins with Evensong of the eve of the feast (first Vespers).

4. The *Common of Saints* may be employed for any of the solemnities, feasts or memorials of Our Lady, the Apostles, Evangelists, Martyrs or other Saints as they occur in the Calendar. On solemnities and feasts what appears in the Common replaces what is found in the Psalter; on memorials a more judicious arrangement is demanded (see page xviii). The Office of the Dead may be used on Nov. 2 and at wakes, funerals and anniversaries. For obvious reasons it is not within the range of this prayer book to provide special materials for any and all the feasts contained in the Roman Calendar.

5. The *Table of Scripture Readings* sets out the new, two-year cycle of longer readings for the Liturgy of the Hours. They may be used to replace the short lessons printed out in the Psalter at either morning or evening worship. If longer lessons are desired both morning and evening, the whole cycle may be used in one year, Year I at Morning Praise, Year II at Evensong. Another possibility is using the "off-year" readings from the Roman Missal. The consistent use of some lectionary or schema is to be preferred to random selection of 'favorite' passages.

With the exception of certain Vigils, the Gospels are not read in the Liturgy of the Hours, since they are arranged to be read each year at Mass. Nevertheless, some communities may find regular Gospel lessons useful or even necessary, particularly if they do not assist at Mass daily. Moreover, since an increased emphasis on the paschal character of the Lord's Day is to be encouraged, the following list of eleven resurrection gospels is recommended for Saturday evenings or Sunday mornings: Mt 28:1–20; Mark 16: 1–8; 16:9–20; Luke 24:1–12; 24:13–35;

24:36–53; John 20:1–10; 20:11–18; 20:19–31; 21:1–14; 21:15–25. Such gospels will, of course, be read with the normal signs of respect due the Gospel. Within the near future appropriate books of homilies and meditations from approved Christian sources will be appearing to supplement the purely Scriptural readings. On occasions, then, there could be a second lesson, morning or evening.

Place of Celebration

The ideal place for celebrating the Hours is, of course, a church or chapel, preferably one without fixed pews facing forward, so that the Office can be celebrated in the midst (*in medio*) of the assembly. Distinct advantages attend the location of the ministers, lectern, etc. *in medio* and facing the altar.

Communities without chapels can often use a dining room or refectory to good advantage. At Evensong, for example, the Light Service and Incense Rite can be carried out very nicely around a table containing a large candle or candelabrum and a stable incense burner. On occasion, it might be appropriate to celebrate those two rites at the beginning of the evening meal and the remainder of Evensong at its end.

How to Pray This Office

Since the basic structure of each Hour is identical, both Hours will be treated together, under seven headings:
1. *Invitatory*
    a. opening versicle and response
    b. hymn
    c. collect or evening thanksgiving
This opening section of the Hour is a call to prayer which gives each day and hour its own liturgical color and, particularly because of the hymn, "makes an easy and pleasant opening to the prayer" (GI, 42).

At Evensong this introductory rite is also a Light Service (*Lucernarium*) celebrating the radiant presence of Jesus Christ, the Light of the World, in the midst of his worshiping people. One of the ministers should carry in or light a large fixed candle in the middle of the assembly. It is his role to sing the opening versicle, to see to the further illumination of the church (if any), and to proclaim the Thanksgiving at the lectern. The more expansive Thanksgivings of Saturday and Sunday evenings are taken from the *Apostolic Constitutions* (Syria, ca. 380 A.D.) and from the *Apostolic Tradition* of St. Hippolytus of Rome (ca. 215 A.D.).

The rubrics in this book speak only of *celebrant* and *assistant minister,* and apply to any who lead the celebration, whether men or women. Some special form of vesture may seem appropriate to the ministers in a celebration of liturgical prayer, e.g., for ordained deacons and priests the normal diaconal and priestly vestments—alb or surplice and stole (on greater feasts dalmatics and copes), or for *cantors* and *readers*—albs or surplices.

2. *Psalmody*

The main body of sung prayer at each Hour consists of three songs:

Morning Praise:
- a. Morning Psalm
- b. Old Testament Canticle
- c. Praise Psalm

Evensong:
- a. Psalm 141 (invariable)
- b. Evening Psalm
- c. New Testament Canticle

After each of these "psalms" the *celebrant* calls the assembly (let us pray) to a period of silent, meditative prayer (kneeling might be an appropriate gesture on ordinary week-days, standing on Sundays and feasts); he concludes the pause with a psalm collect. The pauses for silent prayer are crucial and should be jealously guarded against erosion.

It is the *cantor's role* to intone and lead the hymns, psalms and canticles. This book makes clear provision for different styles of psalmody: antiphonal, choir answering choir verse by verse or strophe by strophe; responsorial, choir answering cantor(s) who carries the burden of the psalmody; metrical, choir answering choir stanza by stanza. Nevertheless, most of these psalms can be performed in more than one way and communities are urged to use their liturgical imagination. (cf. pp. 14–16)

At Evensong the repeated refrain to Psalm 141, the liberal incensation of the congregation by the assistant minister, and the use of special collects accentuate the penitential significance of this highly traditional vesperal psalm. It becomes an evening act of contrition for the sins of the past day and a plea for protection during the night. In this instance incense is an atonement symbol, as in Numbers 16:16–18. For Christians incense can help recall "the sweet odor of Jesus Christ" (II Cor 2:14–16) which penetrates the lives of those who accept him as Lord and Savior. As a purifier and sweetener, incense is an expressive sign of him "who gives himself up in our place as a fragrant offering and sacrifice to God" (Eph 5:2). Among Eastern Christians this kind of incensation is considered a kind of non-verbal 'absolution.'

During the singing of Psalm 141 the assistant minister should:

a. present the censer to the celebrant (if he be an ordained minister) to bless;

b. incense the large candle or candelabrum from all sides;

c. incense the celebrant and other ministers;

d. incense every participant so far as possible so that each might take the blest smoke in his hand, as it were, and bless himself with it as a symbolic way of laying hold of the purifying grace of the evening offering.

When not in active use the censer should stand *in medio*.

3. *Readings*

Whether short or long, the scriptural readings should be proclaimed from the lectern by a *reader* in as clear and intelligible a manner as possible. Patristic and sanctoral readings should supplement and never replace the Bible. A brief homily will often prove a useful adjunct to the reading(s). In smaller groups, more than one person might want to say a word or two about what has just been read. Whatever its form, the homily should not usurp a period of silent reflection on the word of God. As is true of the psalmody, the most important moment in communal prayer is not when the group reads and sings but when, of set purpose, it keeps quiet in order to listen to God speak.

If the Gospels are read during the Office, all stand as usual, make the customary signs of the cross and employ the acclamations used at Mass.

4. *Gospel Canticle*

The time-honored and popular custom of the Roman Church is to employ the Gospel canticles of Zechariah, Mary and Simeon as the pre-eminent acts of praise and thanksgiving (*berakoth*) in each day's Office. Antiphons for the first two "vary according to the liturgical day, season or feast." (GI, 50)

"The Gospel canticles . . . should be accorded the same solemnity and dignity as is usual for the hearing of the Gospel." (GI, 138, 261, 266) This means standing posture, signs of the cross and the incensation of the altar and people. In this instance, the altar is honored with incense to express our belief and our actual participation in the Communion of Saints (Rev 8:3–4). Such incensations are particularly expressive acts of homage on Sundays and solemnities.

The Canticle of Simeon (*Nunc Dimittis*) is one of the most ancient components of evening prayer and, thematically, one of the most fitting for ending another "day of the Lord." (Origen) It is provided as an alternate to the canticle of Mary, especially for those days and seasons when Evensong is celebrated well after sunset, i.e., as night prayer more than as evening prayer. Whenever two readings are used, the Marian canticle could serve after the first reading and that of Simeon after the second.

5. *Corporate Intercessions*

From New Testament times on, universal intercession for the Church and the world has been a basic and customary part of all liturgical prayer (cf. I Tim 2:1–4). Such prayers of intercession were normally framed in a way to permit and encourage the people to play the major role in them. A *deacon* would propose a series of catholic intentions for prayer, while the *people* would steadily repeat a well-known refrain (*Kyrie, eleison*). In such a style it is not so much the announced intentions of the deacon which constitute the prayer, but the repeated, sustained invocations of the people.

This litany mode is employed exclusively at Evensong; the harmonized "Lord, have mercy" is designed to bring out the popular and prayer element of such litanies. Towards the end the *assistant minister/cantor* should suspend his proclamation of intentions and allow a fairly extended time for silent and spontaneous prayer before he finishes with "Rejoicing in the fellowship. . . ." Concluding the litany with a collect is the function of the *celebrant*.

At Morning Praise some forms of intercession are used which imitate the *preces* of the old Roman Breviary.

Kneeling seems appropriate to litanies on plain weekdays.

6. *The Lord's Prayer*

Our Lord's own model prayer is the only fitting conclusion to our communal liturgy of praise and petition. It is "an epitome of the entire Gospel" (Tertullian). It is sung standing.

7. *Blessing*

The celebrant's blessing is not a mere appendage to the service but a form of dismissal which invokes in a conclusive way the power of God on the assembly and sends it away under the shadow of this power.

The blessing is a development and adaptation of the standard Aaronic form (Num 6:23–26) and varies with the day and season. Its final petition for peace may signal a general "kiss of peace" to seal this liturgy of worship and of Christian fellowship.

Ordained ministers give the blessing with extended hands and sign the congregation with the cross; *lay leaders* may use deprecative forms. All bow during the blessings as the assistant minister specifically indicates at Evensong.

Celebrating Prayer in Song

This book of morning and evening prayer has been edited in the hope that these "hinge" hours of the church's prayer will be communally celebrated. A prime consideration has been that of providing music for community prayer.

1. *The music in this book*

For the sake of variety and interest, the psalms, hymns and prayers have been set to several different types of music: hymns and metrical psalms and canticles to chorale tunes, folksong and plainsong; psalms and canticles to Gregorian psalm-tones, chant-type formulae and "Gelineau" style psalm formulae; prayers and litanies to simple melodic formulae. All the music can be sung without instruments. Full harmony is printed for those hymns and metrical psalms whose music is suitable for both SATB performance and organ accompaniment. A few of the refrains (e.g., to the New Testament canticles) and litany-responses are also provided with *ad libitum* harmonizations. Thus, where harmonization is given, it may be used if so desired. Where no harmonization is provided, participants should feel free to add harmony if they so wish.

An important point to remember is that everything in this book may be sung without accompaniment. Accompaniment on organ or guitar, as well as vocal harmonization, may be used where necessary or to provide color and variety for prayer. No one should feel bound to exactly what is presented here. The editors have tried to provide a basic musical structure for the whole of morning and evening prayer and devoutly hope that the creative talents of those who use the book will be whetted by what is here presented. The only *caveat* that should be remembered is this: musical enrichment must always contribute to the *prayer* of the particular community that is celebrating prayer together.

2. *Types of celebration: participants*

This book may be used by large or small groups, men, women or a mixed congregation. The size and skill of a group, as well as the regularity with which they gather for prayer, will determine the way that this book is used. In its simplest form of celebration, one cantor or chantress is needed, in order to intone the music and sing the verses of the psalms. If the prayers, versicles and litanies are also to be sung, the celebrant (male or female) must be able to negotiate the simple medodic formulae that are provided.

Thus, for example, if morning or evening prayer is celebrated by a relatively large congregation in a parish—and one that gathers only on occasion—a strong and competent leader of song is necessary (as well, perhaps, as an organist to accompany the hymns and metrical psalms). In a very small group, e.g., 6–15 participants, only one cantor is necessary. The music can be easily sung by large or small groups once the cantor has sung it through.

Beyond this, much variety is possible. The celebrant may have an assistant (a deacon or quasi-deacon) who would sing the litanies and evening light-preface. Two cantors may be used to alternate verses of psalms (e.g., the verses of the New Testament canticles). The whole group may take the place of the chanters and alternate the psalm verses (if the music is suitable for this) and stanzas of hymns and metrical psalms (particularly, when there are a number of stanzas).

Each group, then, must make a decision before they celebrate morning and evening prayer: how are we going to do it? As indicated above, the book envisages the simplest form of celebration and, perhaps, the most useful: cantor and celebrant, but many other methods of performance are *a propos*.

3. *Further possibilities.*

No one should feel limited to the music in this book; nor is it necessary that everything always be sung. Many styles of music are given (even for the same psalms or canticles; e.g., the *Magnificat, Benedictus* and *Nunc Dimittis* in both a metrical and a psalm setting). But some may have other musical settings they prefer to use at times. This is perfectly in accord with the intentions of the editors of this book. Again, of the psalms presented for a particular day, some communities may prefer the reading of one of them by an individual or the whole group and, sometimes, even accompanied in their reading by a musical instrument. This is particularly suitable when a different translation of the psalms, one more suitable for spoken recitation, is used.

Thus, much variety is possible. The editors have tried to design a book that puts all the necessary materials into the hands of the participants. From these efforts, another *caveat* emerges. It was stated above that any music used should be suitable for community prayer, with the emphasis on *prayer*. A very practical consideration may be added to this: when other materials are used, they should be readily available to the participants in order that the latter may pray conveniently and not be surprised by sudden, unexpected or unusual changes.

The Calendar

The Celebration of The Saints

The celebrations of the saints are arranged in such a way that they do not take precedence over the mysteries of salvation as commemorated on festive days and during the major seasons of the year, and so that they do not continually interfere with the sequence of the psalms and readings, or give rise to unnecessary repetitions. The purpose of this is also to give everyone ample opportunity for legitimate devotion. (GI, 218)

The festival of a saint is either a solemnity, a feast or a memorial:

1. *Solemnities* (S) begin with Evensong of the preceding day (First Vespers). The appropriate Common is combined with the Sunday Psalter; proper collects are available in the Roman Missal. Only solemnities are transferable; see a current calendar.

2. *Feasts* (F) do not have first Vespers. The appropriate Common is combined with the psalms of the current weekday; proper collects are available in the Roman Missal.

3. *Memorials* (M) are lesser feasts and should not be used indiscriminately. As a rule the current Scripture readings in the lectionary should be preferred to the lessons from the Common, especially on optional memorials and those of lesser interest. At times only a small portion of the Common, e.g., the antiphons of the Gospel canticles and the collects, might be used with the Psalter of the day. Certain communities will want to celebrate a given memorial more festively, e.g., Franciscans the feasts of St. Francis and St. Clare.

Memorials are *not* celebrated on Sundays, from Dec. 17–24, during Lent, Holy Week or Easter Week.

The Calendar

January   1   Octave of Christmas
SOLEMNITY OF MARY, MOTHER OF GOD   S
2   Basil the Great and Gregory Nazianzen, bishops and doctors   M
4   Blessed Elizabeth Ann Seton   M
5   Blessed John Neumann, bishop   M
6   [EPIPHANY SOL] +
7   *Raymond of Penyafort, priest*
13   *Hilary, bishop and doctor*
17   Anthony, abbot   M
20   *Fabian, pope and martyr*
Sebastian, martyr
21   Agnes, virgin and martyr   M
22   *Vincent, deacon and martyr*
24   Francis de Sales, bishop and doctor   M
25   Conversion of Paul, apostle   F
26   Timothy and Titus, bishops   M
27   *Angela Merici, virgin*
28   Thomas Aquinas, priest and doctor   M
31   John Bosco, priest   M
Sunday after Epiphany: Baptism of the Lord   F
+   In the United States and Canada Epiphany is celebrated on the first Sunday after Jan. 1.

February   2   Presentation of the Lord   F
3   *Blaise, bishop and martyr*
Ansgar, bishop
5   Agatha, virgin and martyr   M
6   Paul Miki and companions, martyrs   M
8   *Jerome Emiliani, priest*
10   Scholastica, virgin   M
11   *Our Lady of Lourdes*
14   Cyril, monk, and Methodius, bishop   M
17   *Seven Founders of the Order of Servites*
21   *Peter Damian, bishop and doctor*
22   Chair of Peter, apostle   F
23   Polycarp, bishop and martyr   M

March	4	*Casimir*
	7	Perpetua and Felicity, martyrs M
	8	*John of God, religious*
	9	*Frances of Rome, religious*
	17	*Patrick, bishop*
	18	*Cyril of Jerusalem, bishop and doctor*
	19	JOSEPH, HUSBAND OF MARY S
	23	*Turibius of Mongrovejo, bishop*
	25	ANNUNCIATION S

April	2	*Francis of Paola, hermit*
	4	*Isidore, bishop and doctor*
	5	*Vincent Ferrer, priest*
	7	John Baptist de la Salle, priest M
	11	*Stanislaus, bishop and martyr*
	13	*Martin I, pope and martyr*
	21	*Anselm, bishop and doctor*
	23	*George, martyr*
	24	*Fidelis of Sigmaringen, priest and martyr*
	25	Mark, evangelist F
	28	*Peter Chanel, priest and martyr*
	29	Catherine of Siena, virgin and doctor
	30	*Pius V, pope*

May	1	*Joseph the Worker*
	2	Athanasius, bishop and doctor M
	3	Philip and James, apostles F
	12	*Nereus and Achilleus, martyrs*
		Pancras, martyr
	14	Matthias, apostle F
	15	*Isidore the Farmer*
	18	*John I, pope and martyr*
	20	*Bernadine of Siena, priest*
	25	*Venerable Bede, priest and doctor*
		Gregory VII, pope
		Mary Magdalene de Pazzi, virgin
	26	Philip Neri, priest M
	27	*Augustine of Canterbury, bishop*
	31	Visitation F
		First Sunday after Pentecost: HOLY TRINITY S
		Second Sunday after Pentecost: CORPUS CHRISTI S

Friday following Second Sunday after Pentecost:
SACRED HEART   S
Saturday following Second Sunday after Pentecost:
(Immaculate Heart of Mary)

June

1 Justin, martyr   M
2 *Marcellinus and Peter, martyrs*
3 Charles Lwanga and companions, martyrs   M
5 Boniface, bishop and martyr   M
6 *Norbert, bishop*
9 *Ephrem, deacon and doctor*
11 Barnabas, apostle   M
13 Anthony of Padua, priest and doctor   M
19 *Romuald, abbot*
21 Aloysius Gonzaga, religious   M
22 *Paulinus of Nola, bishop*
John Fisher, bishop and martyr, and Thomas More,
martyr
24 BIRTH OF JOHN THE BAPTIST   S
27 *Cyril of Alexandria, bishop and doctor*
28 Irenaeus, bishop and martyr   M
29 PETER AND PAUL, apostles   S
30 *First Martyrs of the Church of Rome*

July

3 Thomas, apostle   F
4 *Elizabeth of Portugal*
5 *Anthony Zaccaria, priest*
6 *Maria Goretti, virgin and martyr*
11 Benedict, abbot   M
13 *Henry*
14 *Camillus de Lellis, priest*
15 Bonaventure, bishop and doctor   M
16 *Our Lady of Mount Carmel*
21 *Lawrence of Brindisi, priest and doctor*
22 Mary Magdalene   M
23 *Bridget, religious*
25 James, apostle   F
26 Joachim and Ann, parents of Mary   M
29 Martha   M
30 *Peter Chrysologus, bishop and doctor*
31 Ignatius of Loyola, priest   M

August	1	Alphonsus Liguori, bishop and doctor	M
	2	*Eusebius of Vercelli, bishop*	
	4	John Vianney, priest	M
	5	*Dedication of Saint Mary Major*	
	6	Transfiguration	F
	7	*Sixtus II, pope and martyr, and companions, martyrs*	
		Cajetan, priest	
	8	Dominic, priest	M
	10	Lawrence, deacon and martyr	F
	11	Clare, virgin	M
	13	*Pontian, pope and martyr, and Hippolytus, priest and martyr*	
	15	ASSUMPTION	S
	16	*Stephen of Hungary*	
	19	*John Eudes, priest*	
	20	Bernard, abbot and doctor	M
	21	Pius X, pope	M
	22	Queenship of Mary	M
	23	*Rose of Lima, virgin*	
	24	Bartholomew, apostle	F
	25	*Louis*	
		Joseph Calasanz, priest	
	27	Monica	M
	28	Augustine, bishop and doctor	M
	29	Beheading of John the Baptist, martyr	M

September	3	Gregory the Great, pope and doctor	M
	8	Birth of Mary	F
	9	Peter Claver, priest	M
	13	John Chrysostom, bishop and doctor	M
	14	Triumph of the Cross	F
	15	Our Lady of Sorrows	M
	16	Cornelius, pope and martyr, and Cyprian, bishop and martyr	M
	17	*Robert Bellarmine, bishop and doctor*	
	19	*Januarius, bishop and martyr*	
	21	Matthew, apostle and evangelist	F
	26	*Cosmas and Damian, martyrs*	
	27	Vincent de Paul, priest	M
	28	*Wenceslaus, martyr*	
	29	Michael, Gabriel and Raphael, archangels	F
	30	Jerome, priest and doctor	M

October	1	Theresa of the Child Jesus, virgin M
	2	Guardian Angels M
	4	Francis of Assisi M
	6	*Bruno, priest*
	7	Our Lady of the Rosary M
	9	*Denis, bishop and martyr, and companions, martyrs*
		John Leonardi, priest
	14	*Callistus I, pope and martyr*
	15	Theresa of Avila, virgin and doctor M
	16	*Hedwig, religious*
		Margaret Mary Alacoque, virgin
	17	Ignatius of Antioch, bishop and martyr M
	18	Luke, evangelist F
	19	Isaac Jogues, priest and martyr, and companions, martyrs M
	23	*John Capistrano, priest*
	24	*Anthony Claret, bishop*
	28	Simon and Jude, apostles F
November	1	ALL SAINTS S
	2	All Souls
	3	*Martin de Porres, religious*
	4	Charles Borromeo, bishop M
	9	Dedication of Saint John Lateran F
	10	Leo the Great, pope and doctor M
	11	Martin of Tours, bishop M
	12	Josaphat, bishop and martyr M
	13	Frances Xavier Cabrini, religious M
	15	*Albert the Great, bishop and doctor*
	16	*Margaret of Scotland*
		Gertrude, virgin
	17	Elizabeth of Hungary, religious M
	18	*Dedication of the churches of Peter and Paul, apostles*
	21	Presentation of Mary M
	22	Cecilia, virgin and martyr M
	23	*Clement I, pope and martyr*
		Columban, abbot
	30	Andrew, apostle F
		Last Sunday of the Year: CHRIST THE KING S
		Fourth Thursday of November (U.S.A.): Thanksgiving Day

December

3 Francis Xavier, priest   M
4 *John Damascene, priest and doctor*
6 *Nicholas, bishop*
7 Ambrose, bishop and doctor   M
8 IMMACULATE CONCEPTION   S
11 *Damasus I, pope*
12 Our Lady of Guadalupe   M
13 Lucy, virgin and martyr   M
14 John of the Cross, priest and doctor   M
21 *Peter Canisius, priest and doctor*
23 *John of Kanty, priest*
25 CHRISTMAS   S
26 Stephen, first martyr   F
27 John, apostle and evangelist   F
28 Holy Innocents, martyrs   F
29 *Thomas Becket, bishop and martyr*
31 *Sylvester I, pope*
Sunday within the octave of Christmas or Dec. 30: Holy Family   F

The Weekly Psalter

"In the Liturgy of the Hours, the Church exercises the priestly office of her head and constantly offers God a sacrifice of praise 'a verbal sacrifice that is offered every time we acknowledge his name.' (Heb 23:15) This prayer is 'the voice of the bride addressing her bridegroom; it is the very prayer which Christ himself, together with his body, addresses to the Father.' . . . By offering praise to God in the Hours, the Church joins in singing that canticle of praise which is sung throughout all ages in the halls of heaven; it is a foretaste of the heavenly praise sung unceasingly before the throne of God and the Lamb. . . .

As well as praising God, the Church's liturgy expresses the hopes and prayers of all the Christian faithful and intercedes before Christ and through him before the Father for the salvation of the whole world . . . and so the Church continues to offer that prayer and entreaty which Christ offered during his life on earth, and which therefore has unique effectiveness."

The General Instruction on the Liturgy of the Hours,
15–16

Sunday—Evensong I

I. Light Service

STAND: The ministers enter, the ASSISTANT MINISTER/ CELEBRANT carrying a lighted candle. Holding the candle up so all can see, he sings:

ASSISTANT: Je - sus Christ is the Light of the world.

ALL: A Light no dark - ness can ex - tin - guish.

As the ASSISTANT MINISTER/CELEBRANT places the candle on its stand, the evening hymn is begun.

EVENING HYMN

O Lux beata Trinitas, c. 6th
Tr. John Mason Neale, 1852, alt.

L.M.

Winchester New, from
Musikalisches Handbuch, Hamburg, 1690

1. O Trin - i - ty, most bless - ed Light, O U - ni - ty of pri - mal Might,
2. To you our morn - ing song of praise To you our eve - ning prayer we raise;
3. To God the Fa - ther glo - ry be, The same, e - ter - nal Son, to thee,

1. As now the fier - y sun de - parts, Im - plant your Light with - in our hearts.
2. O may our sup - pliant glo - ry be To sing your praise e - ter - nal - ly.
3. The Par - a - clete we now a - dore With joy - ful praise for ev - er - more.

THANKSGIVING—Apostolic Constitutions, c. 380

After the evening hymn the ASSISTANT MINISTER/CELE-BRANT stands at the lectern and sings:

ASSISTANT: The Lord be with you. ALL: And al - so with you. ASSISTANT: Let us praise and

thank the Lord. ALL: It is right and fit - ting, for great-ness, mag - nif - i - cence and

glo - ry be - long to him. ASSISTANT: We praise and thank you, O God, for you are

with -out be - gin - ning and with - out end; through Christ you are the Cre - a - tor and

Pre-serv -er of the whole world, but a - bove all you are his God and Fa -ther, the

Giv - er of the Spir - it, and the Rul - er of all that is seen and un - seen. You made

the day for the works of light and the night for the re - fresh-ment of our weak -

ness. O lov - ing Lord and Source of all that is good, mer - ci - ful - ly ac - cept our

ev' - ning sac - ri - fice of praise. As you have con - duct - ed us through the day and

brought us to night's be - gin -ning, keep us now in Christ, grant us a peace-ful

ev' -ning and a night free from sin, and at the end bring us to ev - er - last - ing

life through Christ our Lord. Through him we of - fer glo - ry, hon - or and wor -ship

to you in the Ho - ly Spir - it, now and al - ways and for ev - er and ev - er.

ALL: A - men.

II. Psalmody

STAND: As Psalm 141 is sung, the CELEBRANT places incense in the thurible and the ASSISTANT MINISTER incenses the candle, the celebrant, the other ministers, and the people.

PSALM 141—An evening prayer for forgiveness and protection

English version: Grail

Peregrinus Tone
Arr. David F. Wright, O.P.

ANTIPHON: My prayers rise like in - cense, my hands like the eve - ning of - f'ring.

1. I have called to you, O Lord; / has-ten to help me Hear my voice when I cry to you. Let my prayer rise be-fore you like in - cense, the raising of my hands, like an evening ob - la - tion.

2. Set a guard ov - ver my mouth, O Lord; keep watch, O Lord, at the door of my lips! Do not turn my heart to things that are wrong, to evil deeds with men who are sin - ners,

3. Never allow me to share in their feast - ing. If a good man strikes or reproves me it is kind - ness; But let the oil of the wicked not a -noint my head. Let my prayer be ever against their mal - ice.

4. To you, Lord God, my eyes are turned: in you I take re-fuge;

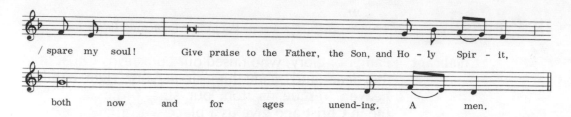

/ spare my soul! Give praise to the Father, the Son, and Ho - ly Spir - it,

both now and for ages unend-ing. A men.

The CELEBRANT begins the prayer immediately.

Celebrant: Father of glory, who raised our Lord Jesus Christ from the dead and made him sit at your right hand in heaven, rescue us from our sins, bring us to new life in Christ and give us a place with him in heaven; through the same Christ Jesus our Lord.

All: Amen.

PSALM 141—Alternate Setting

James Quinn, S.J.
1969

S.M.

Southwell
Damon's *Psalter*, 1579

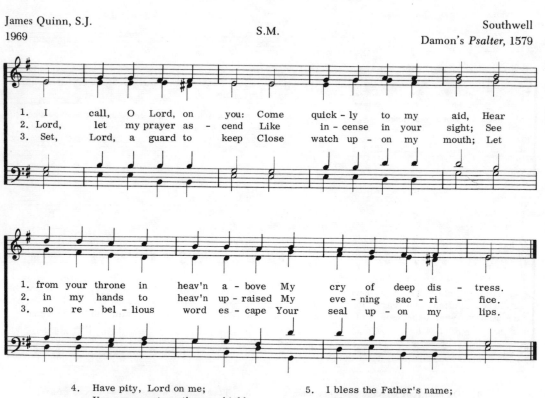

1. I call, O Lord, on you: Come quick - ly to my aid, Hear
2. Lord, let my prayer as - cend Like in - cense in your sight; See
3. Set, Lord, a guard to keep Close watch up - on my mouth; Let

1. from your throne in heav'n a - bove My cry of deep dis - tress.
2. in my hands to heav'n up - raised My eve - ning sac - ri - fice.
3. no re - bel - lious word es - cape Your seal up - on my lips.

4. Have pity, Lord on me;
   You are my strength, my shield:
   You are my refuge in all ills;
   I turn in trust to you.

5. I bless the Father's name;
   I bless the Savior-Son;
   I bless the Spirit of their love,
   My solace in distress.

The CELEBRANT begins the prayer immediately.

Celebrant: Father of glory, who raised our Lord Jesus Christ from the dead and made him sit at your right hand in heaven, rescue us from our sins, bring us to new life in Christ and give us a place with him in heaven; through the same Christ Jesus our Lord.

All: Amen.

The people may sit or stand during the remaining psalmody; they stand, however, for the collects.

PSALM 8—The grandeur of God and the dignity of the Son of Man

The Psalter, 1912, alt.

C.M.

St. Bernard
Cologne, 1741

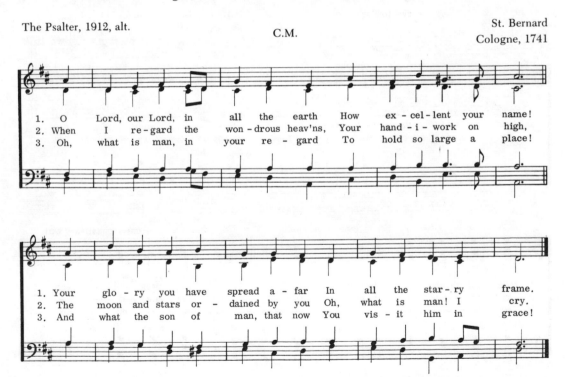

1. O Lord, our Lord, in all the earth How ex-cel-lent your name!
2. When I re-gard the won-drous heav'ns, Your hand-i-work on high,
3. Oh, what is man, in your re-gard To hold so large a place!

1. Your glo-ry you have spread a-far In all the star-ry frame.
2. The moon and stars or-dained by you Oh, what is man! I cry.
3. And what the son of man, that now You vis-it him in grace!

4. On man your wisdom you bestowed
   A pow'r well-nigh divine;
   With honor you have crowned his head
   With glory like to thine.

5. Your mighty works and wondrous grace
   Your glory, Lord, proclaim.
   O Lord, our Lord, in all the earth
   How excellent your name!

Celebrant: Let us pray:

Pause for silent prayer.

O God, whose name is blessed from sunrise to sunset, fill our hearts with knowledge of you and make us worthy to sing your praise and thank you for your great glory, that you may be honored and glorified from east to west and from pole to pole for all the ages of ages; through Jesus Christ our Lord.

All: Amen.

PHILIPPIANS 2:6–11—The humility and exaltation of Christ our Paschal Lamb

English version: NAB   Frank Quinn, O.P.

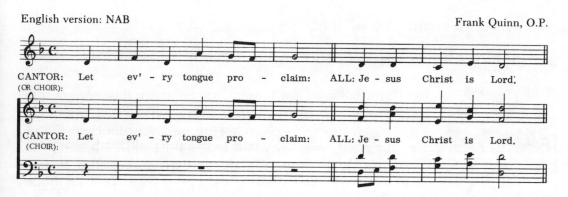

CANTOR: Let ev'-ry tongue pro-claim: ALL: Je-sus Christ is Lord.
(OR CHOIR):

CANTOR: Let ev'-ry tongue pro-claim: ALL: Je-sus Christ is Lord.
(CHOIR):

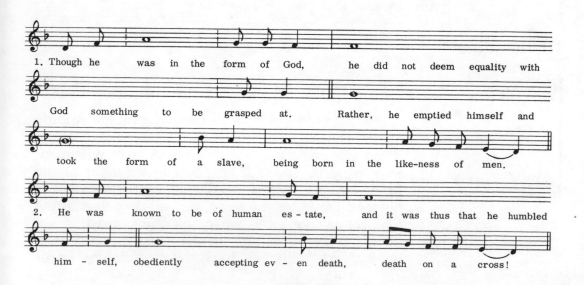

1. Though he was in the form of God, he did not deem equality with God something to be grasped at. Rather, he emptied himself and took the form of a slave, being born in the like-ness of men.

2. He was known to be of human es-tate, and it was thus that he humbled him-self, obediently accepting ev-en death, death on a cross!

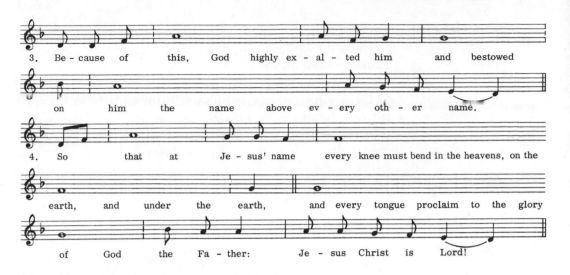

3. Be - cause of this, God highly ex - al - ted him and bestowed on him the name above ev - ery oth - er name.

4. So that at Je - sus' name every knee must bend in the heavens, on the earth, and under the earth, and every tongue proclaim to the glory of God the Fa - ther: Je - sus Christ is Lord!

Celebrant: Let us pray.

Pause for silent prayer

Lord Jesus Christ, who for us men descended into the womb of the Virgin Mary, who hung upon the wood of the cross, whose hands and feet were torn by nails, who was laid in the dust of death and who rose again from the dead, curb our proud hearts, teach us true humility and cause us to rest our hope in you, both now and for ever.

All: Amen.

III. Reading

SIT:

A reading from the letter of blessed Paul the Apostle to the Galatians (6:7–10): Make no mistake about it, no one makes a fool of God! A man will reap only what he sows. If he sows in the field of the flesh, he will reap a harvest of corruption; but if his seed-ground is the spirit, he will reap everlasting life. Let us not grow weary of doing good; if we do not relax our efforts, in due time we shall reap our harvest. While we have the opportunity, let us do good to all men—but especially those of the household of the faith. This is the word of the Lord.

All: Thanks be to God.

A period of silent reflection or brief homily follow. On special days another reading may be added.

IV. Gospel Canticle

CANTICLE OF MARY

STAND: On Sundays and Solemnities when the Canticle of Mary is used, the CELEBRANT places incense in the thurible, and incenses the altar; the ASSISTANT MINISTER then incenses the people.

English version: ICET   Frank Quinn, O.P.

ANTIPHON: Of his king-ship there will be no end.

1. My soul pro-claims the great-ness of the Lord, my spirit rejoices in God my Sav-ior; for he has looked with favor on his low-ly ser-vant, and from this day all generations will call me bless-ed.

2. The Al-mighty has done great things for me: + holy is his Name. He has mercy on those who fear him in every gen-er-a-tion. He has shown the strength of his arm, he has scattered the proud in their con-ceit.

3. He has cast down the mighty from their thrones, and has lifted

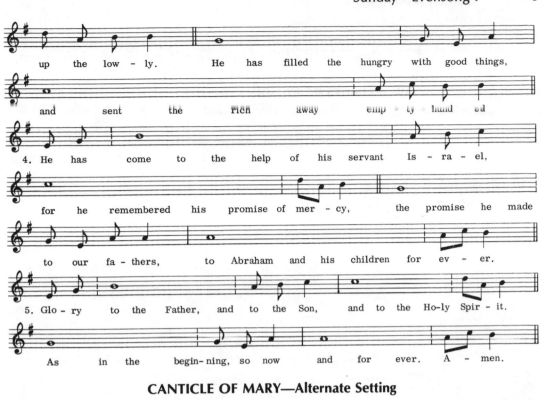

up the low - ly. He has filled the hungry with good things,

and sent the rich away emp - ty hand - ed.

4. He has come to the help of his servant Is - ra - el,

for he remembered his promise of mer - cy, the promise he made

to our fa - thers, to Abraham and his children for ev - er.

5. Glo - ry to the Father, and to the Son, and to the Ho-ly Spir - it.

As in the begin-ning, so now and for ever. A - men.

CANTICLE OF MARY—Alternate Setting

Mein' Seel', O Gott, muss loben dich
Author Unknown, 1535, cento
Tr. J. T. Mueller, 1940, alt.

L.M.

Spires
J. Klug's *Geistliche Lieder*,
1543

1. My soul gives glo - ry to the Lord; In
2. Hence - forth all men shall call me blest, For
3. His mer - cy goes to all who fear, From

1. God my sav - ior I re - joice. My low - li - ness he
2. He has done great things for me. Of all great names his
3. age to age and to all parts. His arm of strength to

<pre>
1. did   re - gard, Ex - alt - ing me by   his own   choice.
2. is   the best, For   it   is ho - ly;   strong is   he.
3. all   is near; He   scat - ters men who   have proud hearts.
</pre>

4. He casts the mighty from their throne
   And raises men of low degree;
   He feeds the hungry as his own;
   The rich depart in poverty.

5. He raised his servant, Israel,
   Rememb'ring his eternal grace,
   As from of old he did foretell
   To Abraham and all his race.

6. O Father, Son, and Spirit blest
   In threefold Name are you adored;
   To you be ev'ry prayer addrest,
   From age to age the only Lord.

Depending upon the feast and the hour of the day, a setting of the Canticle of Simeon might replace the Canticle of Mary.

CANTICLE OF SIMEON

English version: Grail, alt.   Frank Quinn, O.P.

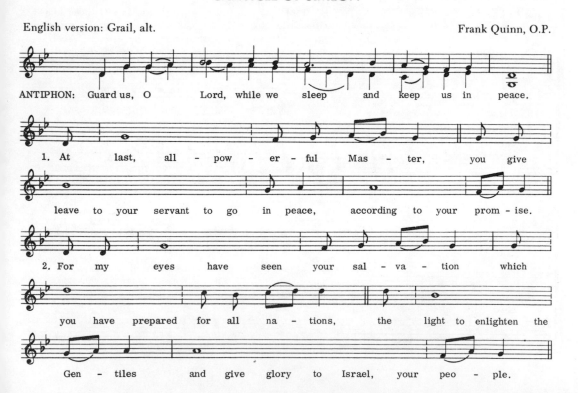

ANTIPHON: Guard us, O Lord, while we sleep and keep us in peace.

1. At last, all-pow-er-ful Mas-ter, you give leave to your servant to go in peace, according to your prom-ise.

2. For my eyes have seen your sal-va-tion which you have prepared for all na-tions, the light to enlighten the Gen-tiles and give glory to Israel, your peo-ple.

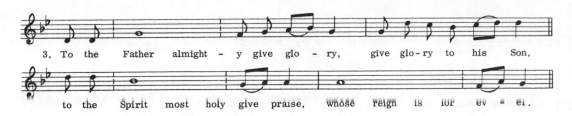

3. To the Father almight - y give glo - ry, give glo-ry to his Son,
to the Spirit most holy give praise, whose reign is for ev - er.

CANTICLE OF SIMEON—Alternate Setting

English version:
Frank Quinn, O.P.

C.M.

Dean, in *Kentucky*
Harmony, 1816

1. My mas-ter, see, the time has come To give your ser-vant leave,
2. For I have seen sal - va-tion, Lord And this may all men see,
3. Al might-y Fa - ther, hear our cry Through Christ the on - ly Son,

1. To go in peace, long wait-ed for Your pro-mise now ful - filled.
2. That light which is your Is-rael's boast En - light-'ning ev - 'ry land.
3. Whom in the Spir-it we a - dore For a - ges with-out end.

V. Intercessions

STAND: The ASSISTANT MINISTER/CANTOR sings the peti-tions, and the people sing the response after each petition.

ASSISTANT: In peace let us pray to the Lord.

R. Lord, have mer - cy.

2. For the holy Church of God that he may give it peace and unity and protect and prosper it throughout the whole world, let us pray to the Lord.

3. For an outpouring of the Spirit on all bishops and other ministers of the Gospel to the greater glory of his name, let us pray to the Lord.

4. For our civil authorities that God may direct their hearts and minds for our lasting peace, let us pray to the Lord.

5. For all who have strayed from Christ's Church that they may return to faith and the obedience of love, let us pray to the Lord.

6. For the Jewish people, the first to hear the word of God, that they may continue in faithfulness to his covenant.

7. For all unbelievers that they may be converted to the true and living God, let us pray to the Lord.

8. For the correction of error, the elimination of disease, famine and war, and for the reconciliation of states and peoples, let us pray to the Lord.

9. For the freeing of prisoners, the healing of the sick, the feeding of the hungry and the consolation of the afflicted, let us pray to the Lord.

10. For those who have gone before us in the discipleship of Christ, let us pray to the Lord.

11. Help, save, pity and defend us, O God, by your grace.

Pause

12. Rejoicing in the fellowship of the Blessed Virgin Mary, of St. *Name,* and of all the saints, let us commend ourselves, one another and our whole life to Christ our Lord.

R: To you, O Lord,

Celebrant: O Lord our God, whose power is beyond compare, whose glory is incomprehensible, whose mercy is measureless and whose love for mankind is beyond words to describe, be pleased in your compassion to look upon us and on this holy place and to grant us and those praying with us the riches of your loving kindness; for all glory, honor and worship are your due, Father, Son and Holy Spirit, now and for ever.

All: Amen.

VI. Lord's Prayer

CELEBRANT: Lord, re-mem-ber us in your king-dom, and teach us to pray.

ALL: Our Fa-ther in heav-en, ho-ly be your name, your king-dom come,

your will be done, on earth as in heav-en. Give us to-day our dai-ly

bread. For-give us our sins as we for-give those who sin a-gainst us.

Do not bring us to the test, but de-liv-er us from e-vil.

For the king-dom, the pow-er, and the glo-ry are yours now and for ev-er.

VII. Blessing and Dismissal

The ASSISTANT MINISTER sings:

ASSISTANT: Bow down your heads to the Lord.

With raised hand the CELEBRANT imparts a blessing.

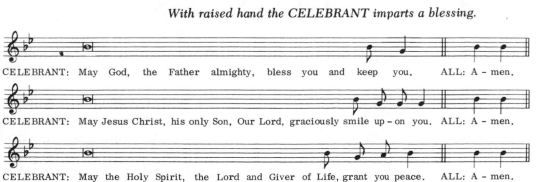

CELEBRANT: May God, the Father almighty, bless you and keep you.   ALL: A - men.

CELEBRANT: May Jesus Christ, his only Son, Our Lord, graciously smile up-on you.   ALL: A - men.

CELEBRANT: May the Holy Spirit, the Lord and Giver of Life, grant you peace.   ALL: A - men.

A sign of peace may be exchanged.

Sunday—Morning Prayer

I. Invitatory

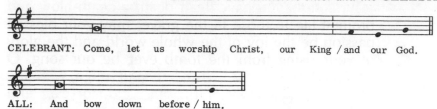

STAND: The ministers enter and the CELEBRANT SINGS:

CELEBRANT: Come, let us worship Christ, our King / and our God.

ALL: And bow down before / him.

MORNING HYMN

Le Mans Breviary, 1748
Tr. H. W. Baker, 1821-77, alt.

77.77

Gott sei dank
Freylinghausen's
Geistreiches Gesangbuch, 1704

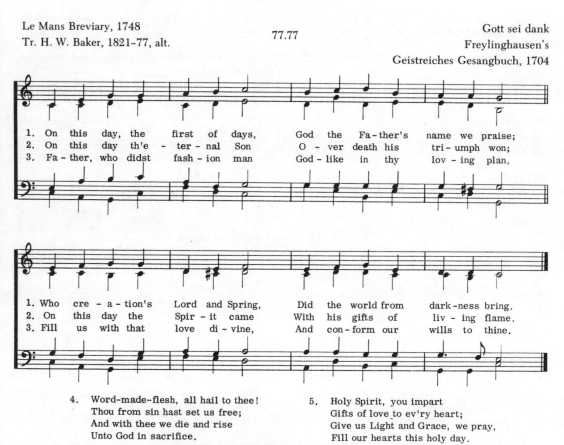

1. On this day, the first of days, God the Fa-ther's name we praise;
2. On this day th'e - ter - nal Son O - ver death his tri - umph won;
3. Fa - ther, who didst fash - ion man God - like in thy lov - ing plan,

1. Who cre - a - tion's Lord and Spring, Did the world from dark-ness bring.
2. On this day the Spir - it came With his gifts of liv - ing flame.
3. Fill us with that love di - vine, And con - form our wills to thine.

4. Word-made-flesh, all hail to thee!
   Thou from sin hast set us free;
   And with thee we die and rise
   Unto God in sacrifice.

5. Holy Spirit, you impart
   Gifts of love to ev'ry heart;
   Give us Light and Grace, we pray,
   Fill our hearts this holy day.

6. God, the blessed Three in One,
   May thy holy will be done;
   In thy word our souls are free,
   And we rest this day with thee.

Celebrant: The Lord be with you.

All: And also with you.

The prayer follows immediately.

Celebrant: Lord Jesus Christ, by your holy cross and your glorious resurrection, you have dealt death a death-blow and brought life to those in the grave; may your blessed passion be the joy of the whole world and the glory of your rising from the tomb ever be our song, O Savior of the world, who live and reign with the Father and the Holy Spirit, one God, for ever and ever.

All: Amen.

II. Psalmody

The people may sit during the first two psalms; they stand, however, for the collects and the Psalm of Praise.

PSALM 63—Longing for God

English version: Grail   Frank Quinn, O.P.

ANTIPHON: In the shad - ow of your wings I re - joice

1. O GOD, / you are my God, + for you I long from / EAR - ly morn ing; *
   My body / PINES for you *

   for you my / soul is THIRST - ing.
   like a dry, weary land / with - out WA - ter.

2. So I gaze on you in the / SANCtuary * to see your strength / and your GLOry.
   For your love is / better than life, * my lips will / SPEAK YOUR praise.

3. So I will bless you / ALL my life, * in your name I will / lift up MY hands.
   My soul shall be filled as / WITH a banquet, * my mouth shall / praise you WITH joy.

4. On my bed I re / MEMber you. * On you I muse / THROUGH THE night.
   For you have / BEEN my help; * in the shadow of your / WINGS I rejoice.

5. My soul / CLINGS to you; * your right / hand holds ME fast.
   Glory to the Father, and to the Son, and to the / HOly Spirit * As in the beginning,
   so now and for / ever. A-men,

Celebrant: Let us pray.

Pause for silent prayer.

From early morning, O Source of undying light, we seek you in your sanctuary, for your love is better than life; may our lips speak your praise, our morning meditation glorify you and our lives be spent in your service; through Jesus Christ our Lord.

All: Amen.

THE CANTICLE OF THE THREE YOUNG MEN (Daniel 3:57–88,56)
I believe in God, the Father almighty, Creator of heaven and earth.

The New American Bible   F. Quinn

ALL: 1. Bless the Lord, all you works of the Lord, An-gels of the Lord, bless the Lord.

2. You heav-ens, bless the Lord, All you wa-ters a-bove the heav-ens bless the Lord, All you hosts of the Lord, bless the Lord; Sun and moon, bless the Lord; ALL: praise and ex-alt him a-bove all for-ev-er.

3. Stars of heav-en, bless the Lord; Ev-ery shower and dew, bless the Lord; All you winds, bless the Lord; ALL: praise and ex-alt him a-bove all for-ev-er.

4. Fire and heat, bless the Lord; Cold and chill, bless the Lord; Dew and rain, bless the Lord; ALL: praise and ex-alt him a-bove all for-ev-er.

5. Frost and chills, bless the Lord; Ice and snow, bless the Lord; Nights and

days, bless the Lord; ALL: praise and ex - alt him a - bove all for - ev - er.

6. Light and dark - ness, bless the Lord; Light - nings and clouds, bless the Lord;

Let the earth bless the Lord; ALL: praise and ex - alt him a - bove all for - ev - er.

7. Moun - tains and hills, bless the Lord; Ev - ery - thing grow - ing from the earth, bless the Lord;

You springs, bless the Lord; ALL: praise and ex - alt him a - bove all for - ev - er.

8. Seas and riv - ers, bless the Lord; You dol - phins and all wa - ter

crea - tures, bless the Lord; All you birds of the air, bless the Lord;

ALL: praise and ex - alt him a - bove all for - ev - er.

9. All you beasts, wild and tame, bless the Lord; You sons of men,

bless the Lord; ALL: praise and ex - alt him a - bove all for - ev - er.

10. O Is - ra - el, bless the Lord; Priests of the Lord, bless the Lord; Ser - vants of the

Lord, bless the Lord; ALL: praise and ex - alt him a - bove all for - ev - er.

11. Spir - its and souls of the just, bless the Lord; Ho - ly men of hum - ble

heart, bless the Lord; Ha - na - ni - ah, A - za - ri - ah, Mish - ael,

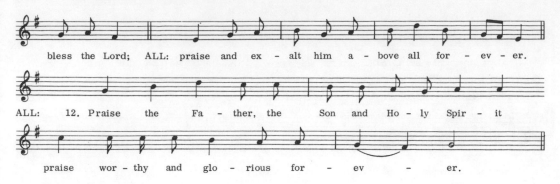

bless the Lord; ALL: praise and ex - alt him a - bove all for - ev - er.

ALL: 12. Praise the Fa - ther, the Son and Ho - ly Spir - it

praise wor - thy and glo - rious for - ev - er.

Celebrant: Let us pray

Pause for silent prayer.

O God, who fashioned the human powers of reasoning and of speech, accept our hymns of praise which we offer as well as we can in union with all creation which sings the praises of your inexpressible glory; for all the powers of heaven praise you and we glorify you, Father, Son and Holy Spirit, now and for ever.

All: Amen.

STAND.

PSALM 150—The Grand Doxology

English version by
David F. Wright, O.P.

L.M.

Illsley
J. Bishop, c. 1665-1737

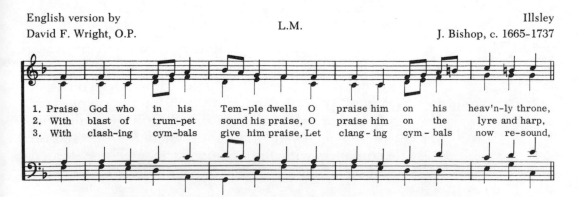

1. Praise God who in his Tem-ple dwells O praise him on his heav'n-ly throne,
2. With blast of trum-pet sound his praise, O praise him on the lyre and harp,
3. With clash-ing cym-bals give him praise, Let clang-ing cym-bals now re-sound,

1. Yes, praise him for his might-y deeds Whose maj - es - ty sur - pass - es all.
2. With tim - brel and in dance give praise, O praise him with the string and reed.
3. Let ev' - ry thing that lives and breathes Give praise to their al - might - y God.

4. All praise to God the Father be,
   To Christ his own beloved Son,
   And to the Spirit, Bond of love,
   The triune God for ever praised.

Celebrant: Let us pray.

Pause for silent prayer.

In union with the great Mother of God, Mary most holy, and with all the saints, we honor and venerate the sacred mysteries of the passion, death and resurrection of our Lord and Savior Jesus Christ; may the unmistakeable perfume of his presence be the fresh fragrance of life itself for us, now and always and for ever and ever.

All: Amen.

III. Reading

SIT

A reading from the first letter of blessed Paul the Apostle to the Corinthians (15:1–8): Brothers, I want to remind you of the gospel, I preached to you, which you received and in which you stand firm. You are being saved by it at this very moment if you hold fast to it as I preached it to you. Otherwise you have believed in vain. I handed on to you first of all what I myself received, that Christ died for our sins in accordance with the Scriptures; that he was buried and, in accordance with the Scriptures, rose on the third day, that he was seen by Cephas, then by the Twelve. After that he was seen by five hundred brothers at once, most of whom are still alive, although some have fallen asleep. Next he was seen by James; then by all the apostles. Last of all he was seen by me, as one born out of the normal course. This is the word of the Lord.

All: Thanks be to God

A period of silent reflection or brief homily follow. On special days another reading may be added.

IV. Gospel Canticle

STAND: On Sundays and Solemnities the CELEBRANT places incense in the thurible, and incenses the altar; the ASSISTANT MINISTER then incenses the people.

CANTICLE OF ZECHARIAH

English version: ICET

Frank Quinn, O.P.

ANTIPHON: I am the al - pha and the o - me - ga, the be - gin - ning and the end, the first and the last.

1. Blest be the Lord, the God of - Is - ra - el; he has come to his peo - ple and set them free. He has raised up for us a might- y sav - ior, born of the house of his ser - vant Da - vid.

2. Through his ho - ly pro-phets he prom-ised of old that he would save us from our en - e - mies, from the hands of all who hate us. He

CANTICLE OF ZECHARIAH—Alternate Setting

James Quinn, S.J.
1969

C.M.D.

Kingsfold

1. Bless'sd be the God of Is - ra - el, The ev - er - liv - ing Lord,
2. Through ho - ly pro-phets did he speak His word to men of old,
3. Of old he swore his sol - emn oath To fa - ther A - bra - ham:

1. Who comes in pow'r to save his own, His peo - ple Is - ra - el.
2. That he would save us from our foes And all who bear us ill.
3. His seed a might - y race should be And bless'd for ev - er - more.

1. For Is - ra - el he rais - es up Sal - va - tion's tow'r on high
2. So to our fa - thers did he give His cov - e - nant of love;
3. He swore to set his peo - ple free From fear of ev - 'ry foe

1. In Da - vid's house, who reigned as king And ser - vant of the Lord.
2. So with their sons he keeps his troth In love that knows no end.
3. That we might serve him all our days In good-ness, love and peace.

4. O tiny child, your name shall be
The prophet of the Lord;
The way of God you shall prepare
To make his coming known.
You shall proclaim to Israel
Salvation's dawning day,
When God shall wipe away men's sins
In his redeeming love.

5. The rising Sun shall shine on us
To bring the light of day
To all who sit in darkest night
And shadow of the grave.
Our footsteps God shall safely guide
To walk the ways of peace.
His name for evermore be bless'd
Who lives and loves and saves.

V. Intercessions

STAND: The ASSISTANT MINISTER/CANTOR sings the petitions, and the people sing the response after each petition.

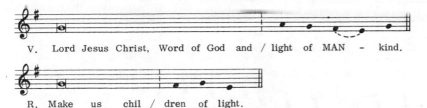

V. Lord Jesus Christ, Word of God and / light of MAN - kind.

R. Make us chil / dren of light.

V: Lord Jesus Christ, only Son of the Father,/full of grace and truth.

R: Make us chil/dren of light.

V: Lord Jesus Christ, chosen Son of God, baptize us in the fire of your/Holy SPIrit.

R: Make us chil/dren of light.

V: Lord Jesus Christ, Savior of the world, teach us to worship the Father in/spirit and in truth.

R: Make us chil/dren of light.

V: Lord Jesus Christ, living bread come down from heaven, raise us up/on the LAST day.

R: Make us chil/dren of light.

Other petitions may be added.

Celebrant: God and Father of our Lord Jesus Christ, of your infinite goodness we are a chosen race, a royal priesthood, a consecrated nation, a people set apart to sing your praises; enable us to live honorably and unselfishly in this world and so arrive at the glories of the celestial city, where in union with all the blessed company of heaven we shall sing of your majestic deeds for ever and ever.

All: Amen.

VI. Lord's Prayer

CELEBRANT: Lord, re-mem-ber us in your king-dom, and teach us to pray.

ALL: Our Fa-ther in heav-en, ho-ly be your name, your king-dom come,

your will be done, on earth as in heav-en. Give us to-day

our dai-ly bread. For-give us our sins as we for-give

those who sin a-gainst us. Do not bring us to the test,

but de-liv-er us from e-vil. For the king-dom,

the pow-er, and the glo-ry are yours now and for ev-er.

VII. Blessing and Dismissal

ASSISTANT: Let us / bless the Lord. ALL: Thanks be to / God.

CELEBRANT: May he who rose from the dead, Christ our true God, bless /

us and keep us. ALL: A - / men.

A sign of peace may be exchanged.

Sunday—Evensong II

I. Light Service

STAND: The ministers enter, the ASSISTANT MINISTER/ CELEBRANT carrying a lighted candle. Holding the candle up so all can see, he sings:

ASSISTANT: Je - sus Christ is the light of the world.

ALL: A light no dark - ness can ex - tin - guish

As the ASSISTANT MINISTER/CELEBRANT places the candle on its stand, the evening hymn is begun.

EVENING HYMN

Lucis Creator optime, 7/8c
Tr. Br. Paul Quenon, O.C.S.O., 1968

L.M.

Tallis' Canon

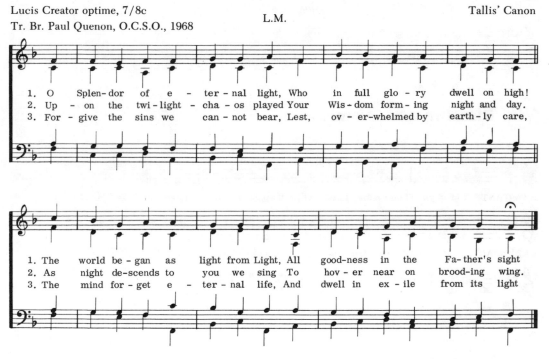

1. O Splen-dor of e - ter-nal light, Who in full glo - ry dwell on high!
2. Up - on the twi - light - cha - os played Your Wis-dom form - ing night and day.
3. For - give the sins we can - not bear, Lest, ov - er-whelmed by earth - ly care,

1. The world be - gan as light from Light, All good-ness in the Fa-ther's sight
2. As night de-scends to you we sing To hov - er near on brood-ing wing.
3. The mind for - get e - ter - nal life, And dwell in ex - ile from its light

4. Let heaven's Spirit pulse within
To purge the memory of sin;
Thus, casting off forgetful night,
We rise enrobed with first-born light.

5. Almighty Father, hear our cry
Through Jesus Christ our Lord most high,
Whom in the Spirit we adore,
Who reigns with you for evermore.

THANKSGIVING—Apostolic Tradition, c. 215

*After the evening hymn the ASSISTANT MINISTER/CELE-
BRANT stands at the lectern and sings:*

ASSISTANT: The Lord be with you. ALL: And al - so with you.

ASSISTANT: Let us praise and thank the Lord. ALL: It is right and fit - ting,

for great - ness, mag - nif - i - cence and glo - ry be - long to him.

ASSISTANT: We praise and thank you, O God, through your Son Je - sus Christ,

our Lord, through whom you have en - light - ened us, by re - veal - ing the

light that nev - er fades. Night is fal - ling, and day's al - lot - ted

span draws to a close. The day - light which you cre - a - ted for our

plea-sure has ful - ly sat - is - fied us; and yet, of your free gift,

now the eve - ning lights do not fail us. We praise you and

glo - ri - fy you through your Son, Je - sus Christ, our Lord; through him be

glo - ry pow - er and hon - or to you and the Ho - ly Spir - it,

now and al - ways and for ev - er and ev - er. ALL: A - men.

II. Psalmody

STAND: As Psalm 141 is sung, the CELEBRANT places incense in the thurible, and the ASSISTANT MINISTER incenses the candle, the celebrant, the other ministers, and the people.

PSALM 141—An evening prayer for forgiveness and protection

ANTIPHON: My prayers rise like in - cense, my hands like the eve - ning of - f'-ring.

Psalm verses: p. 3. After the psalm is completed the CELEBRANT begins the prayer immediately.

Celebrant: Heavenly Father, accept the incense of our repentant prayer, blot out our sins and make us temples of your Holy Spirit, that we may watch and pray for the coming of our Lord Jesus Christ in glory; his kingdom will endure through all the ages of ages.

All: Amen.

The people may sit or stand during the remaining psalmody, they stand, however, for the collects.

PSALM 23
"The Lamb on the throne will shepherd them." (Rev 7:17)

English version: Paul Francis　　　　　　　　　　　　　　　Russell Woollen

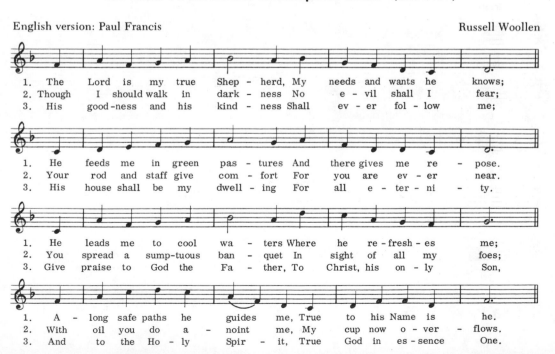

1. The Lord is my true Shep - herd, My needs and wants he knows;
2. Though I should walk in dark - ness No e - vil shall I fear;
3. His good-ness and his kind - ness Shall ev - er fol - low me;

1. He feeds me in green pas - tures And there gives me re - pose.
2. Your rod and staff give com - fort For you are ev - er near.
3. His house shall be my dwell - ing For all e - ter - ni - ty.

1. He leads me to cool wa - ters Where he re - fresh - es me;
2. You spread a sump-tuous ban - quet In sight of all my foes;
3. Give praise to God the Fa - ther, To Christ, his on - ly Son,

1. A - long safe paths he guides me, True to his Name is he.
2. With oil you do a - noint me, My cup now o - ver - flows.
3. And to the Ho - ly Spir - it, True God in es - sence One.

Celebrant: Let us pray.

Pause for silent prayer.

Lighten our darkness, O Lord, and by your great mercy defend us from all perils and dangers of this night, for the love of your only Son our Savior Jesus Christ, who lives and reigns with you and the Holy Spirit for ever and ever.

All: Amen.

CANTICLE FOR ALL SEASONS OUTSIDE OF LENT
REVELATION 19: 1, 2a, 5b–8—The marriage of the Lamb

Verses should be taken by two cantors or two choirs (if possible); one alleluia is added after the first half of the verse, two at the conclusion, and three at the end of the doxology. See optional harmony for these at the end of the canticle.

English version: NAB   Frank Quinn, O.P.

1a. Sal - va - tion, glo - ry and might be - long to our God.

ALL: Al - le - le - lu - ia.

1b. for his judge - ments are true and just.

ALL: Al - le - lu - ia, al - le - lu - ia.

2a. Praise our God, all you ser - vants:

ALL: Al - le - lu - ja.

2b. the small and the great, who re - vere him.

ALL: Al – le – lu – ia, al – le – lu – ia.

3a. The Lord is king, our God, the Al – might – y!

ALL: Al – le – lu – ia.

3b. Let us re – joice and be glad, and give him glo – ry!

ALL: Al – le – lu – ia, al – le – lu – ia.

4a. For this is the wed – ding day of · the Lamb;

ALL: Al – le – lu – ia.

4b. his bride has pre – pared her – self for the wed – ding.

ALL: Al – le – lu – ia, al – le – lu – ia.

5a. She has been giv – en a dress to wear

ALL: Al – le – lu – ia.

5b. made of fin – est lin – en, bril – liant white.

ALL: Al – le – lu – ia, al – le – lu – ia.

6a. Glo – ry to the Fa – ther, and to the Son, and to the Ho – ly Spir – it.

ALL: Al - le - lu - ia.

6b. As   in the be-gin-ning, so   now and for   ev - er.   A - men!

ALL: Al - le - lu - ia, al - le - lu - ia,   al - le - lu - ia.

Formula for canticle and harmonized alleluias:

1st part of verse: ALL: Al - le - lu - ia.

Conclusion of verse: ALL: Al - le - lu - ia, al - le - lu - ia!

Final triple alleluia:

A - men. ALL: Al - le - lu - ia, al - le - lu - ia,   al - le - lu - ia!

Celebrant: Let us pray.

Pause for silent prayer

Lord Jesus Christ, faithful witness and first-born from the dead, ruler of the kings of the earth, wash away our sins in your blood and make us a line of kings and priests to serve your God and Father, now and for ever.

All: Amen.

CANTICLE FOR THE SEASON OF LENT

1 PETER 2:21–24—Jesus the suffering servant of God.

English version: NAB   Frank Quinn, O.P.

ANTIPHON:
By his wounds we have been healed.

ANTIPHON:
harmony
By his wounds we have been healed.

1. Christ suffered for you and left you an ex - am - ple,
to have you fol - low in his foot - steps.

2. He did no wrong; no de - ceit was found in his mouth.
When he was in - sul - ted, he re - turned no in - sult.

3. When he was made to suf - fer, he did not coun - ter with threats.
In - stead he de - liv - ered him - self up to the One who judg - es just - ly.

4. In his own bo - dy he brought your sins to the cross, so that all of us,
dead to sin, could live in ac - cord with God's will. By his wounds you were healed.

5. At one time you were stray - ing like sheep, but now you have

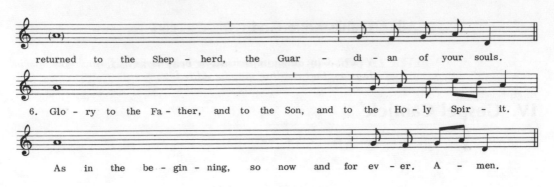

returned   to   the   Shep - herd,   the   Guar - di - an   of   your   souls.

6. Glo - ry to the Fa - ther, and to the Son, and to the Ho - ly Spir - it.

As   in   the   be - gin - ning,   so   now   and   for ev - er.   A - men.

Celebrant: Let us pray.

Pause for silent prayer

Lord Jesus Christ, faithful witness and first-born from the dead, ruler of the kings of the earth, wash away our sins in your blood and make us a line of kings and priests to serve your God and Father, now and for ever.

All: Amen.

III. Reading

SIT

A reading from the first letter of blessed Paul the Apostle to Timothy (6:11–16): Man of God that you are . . . seek after integrity, piety, faith, love, steadfastness, and a gentle spirit. Fight the good fight of faith. Take firm hold on the everlasting life to which you were called when, in the presence of many witnesses, you made your noble profession of faith. Before God, who gives life to all, and before Christ Jesus, who in bearing witness made his noble profession before Pontius Pilate, I charge you to keep God's command without blame or reproach until our Lord Jesus Christ shall appear. This appearance God will bring to pass at his chosen time. He is the blessed and only ruler, the King of kings and Lord of lords who alone has immortality and who dwells in unapproachable light, whom no human being has ever seen or can see. To him be honor and everlasting rule! Amen. This is the word of the Lord.

All: Thanks be to God.

A period of silent reflection or brief homily follow. On special days another reading may be added.

IV. Gospel Canticle

STAND

CANTICLE OF MARY

ANTIPHON: You   are   the   Christ,   the   Son   of   the   liv - ing God.

Verses of the Canticle: p. 8. The alternate setting of the Canticle may be used, or one of the settings of the Canticle of Simeon.

V. Intercessions

STAND: The ASSISTANT MINISTER/CANTOR sings the petitions, and the people sing the response after each petition.

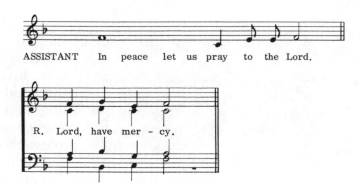

ASSISTANT   In   peace   let   us   pray   to   the   Lord.

R. Lord, have mer - cy.

2. For peace from on high and the salvation of our souls, let us pray to the Lord.

3. For peace throughout the world, the welfare of the holy churches of God and the unity of mankind, let us pray to the Lord.

4. For this holy place (or assembly) and for those who enter it with faith, reverence and fear of God, let us pray to the Lord.

5. For our holy father . . ., for our bishop . . ., the reverend order of priests, the deacons who serve in Christ and for all the clergy and people, let us pray to the Lord.

6. For this nation, its government and all who serve and protect us, let us pray to the Lord.

7. For this city and for every city and country and for all those living in them, let us pray to the Lord.

8. For seasonable weather, bountiful harvests and for peaceful times, let us pray to the Lord.

9. For the safety of travellers, the recovery of the sick, the deliverance of the oppressed and the release of captives, let us pray to the Lord.

10. For our deliverance from all affliction, hostility, danger and need, let us pray to the Lord.

11. Help, save, pity and defend us, O God, by your grace. *(Pause)*

12. Rejoicing in the fellowship of the Blessed Virgin Mary, of St. *Name* and of all the saints, let us commend ourselves, one another and our whole life to Christ Our Lord.

R: To you, O Lord.

Celebrant: By your grace, O Lord, we make these common prayers with one accord, holding to your promise that you will grant the requests of two or three gathered together in your name; fulfil now, O Lord, the petitions of your people as may be most expedient for them, granting us in this world knowledge of your truth and in the world to come life everlasting; for all glory, honor and worship are your due, Father, Son and Holy Spirit, now and for ever.

All: Amen.

VI. Lord's Prayer

CELEBRANT: Lord, re - mem - ber   us   in   your   king - dom,   and   teach   us   to   pray.

ALL: Our Fa - ther in heav - en, ho - ly be your name, your king - dom come,

your will be done, on earth as in heav - en. Give us to - day

our dai - ly bread. For - give us our sins as we for give those who

sin a - gainst us. Do not bring us to the test,

but de - liv - er us from e - vil. For the king - dom,

the pow - er, and the glo - ry are yours now and for ev - er.

VII. Blessing and Dismissal

The ASSISTANT MINISTER sings:

ASSISTANT: Bow down your heads to the Lord.

With raised hand the CELEBRANT imparts a blessing.

CELEBRANT: May the risen Christ bless you and keep you.   ALL: A - men.

CELEBRANT: May the Savior of the world graciously smile up - on you.   ALL: A - men.

CELEBRANT: May the Lord grant you peace.   ALL: A - men.

A sign of peace may be exchanged.

Monday—Morning Prayer

I. Invitatory

STAND

CELEBRANT: Blessed be our God at all times. ALL: Now and for ever. A-men.

MORNING HYMN

Psalm 95
The Psalter, 1912, alt.

C.M.

Dunfermline
Scottish Psalter, 1615

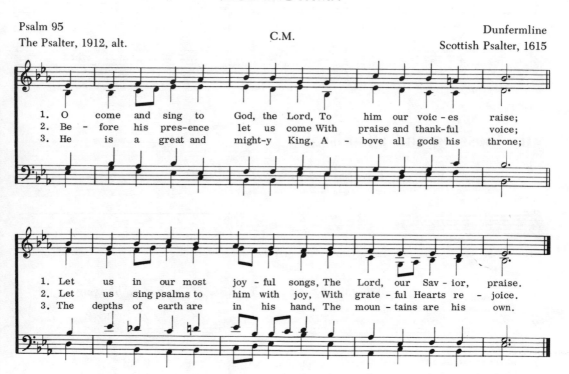

1. O come and sing to God, the Lord, To him our voic-es raise;
2. Be-fore his pres-ence let us come With praise and thank-ful voice;
3. He is a great and might-y King, A-bove all gods his throne;

1. Let us in our most joy-ful songs, The Lord, our Sav-ior, praise.
2. Let us sing psalms to him with joy, With grate-ful Hearts re-joice.
3. The depths of earth are in his hand, The moun-tains are his own.

4. To him the spacious sea belongs,
   He made its waves and tides;
   And by his hand the rising land
   Was formed, and still abides.

5. O Come, and bowing down to him
   Our worship let us bring;
   Yes, let us kneel before the Lord,
   Our Maker and our King.

Celebrant: The Lord be with you.

All: And also with you.

The prayer follows immediately.

Celebrant: Lord Jesus Christ, radiant light of God's glory and perfect image of his nature, make your teaching our rule of life and bring us into all truth as you have promised, O Savior of the world, who live and reign for ever and ever.

All: Amen.

II. Psalmody

The people may sit during the first two psalms; they stand, however, for the collects and the Psalm of Praise.

PSALM 19A—Praise of the Creator

English version: Grail

Frank Quinn, O.P.

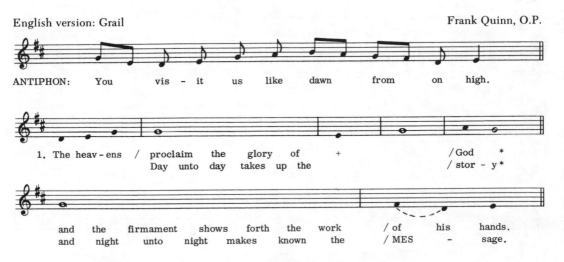

ANTIPHON: You vis - it us like dawn from on high.

1. The heav - ens / proclaim the glory of + / God *
   Day unto day takes up the / stor - y *

   and the firmament shows forth the work / of his hands.
   and night unto night makes known the / MES - sage.

2. No speech, no word, no voice is / heard + yet their span goes forth through all the / earth, *
   their words to the utmost bounds / of the world. *
   There he has placed a tent for the / sun; + it comes forth like a bridegroom coming from his / tent, *
   rejoices like a champion to / run its course.

3. At the end of the sky is the rising of the / sun; + to the furthest end of the sky is its / course. *
   There is nothing concealed from its / burning heat.
   Glory to the Father, and to the Son, and to the Holy / Spirit: *
   As in the beginning, so now and for ev / er. A - men.

Celebrant: Let us pray.

Pause for silent prayer.

Creator of the morning, who scatters the darkness and brings light and joy to creation, create in us habits of virtue and scatter the darkness of sin by the glorious rays of your grace; through Jesus Christ our Lord.

All: Amen.

1 CHRONICLES 29:10–13—Christ the Lord reigns over all

English version: NAB   Frank Quinn, O.P.

ANTIPHON: God has blessed us, with all spir - it - ual bless - ing in Christ.

1. Blessed may you be, O Lord, God of Israel our fa - ther,

from   eternity   to e - ter - ni - ty.

2. Yours, O Lord, are grandeur and power, majesty, splendor,

and glo - ry. For all in heaven and on earth is yours;

3. yours, o Lord, is the sover - eign - ty; you are exalted as head o - ver all.

Riches and honor are from you, and you have do - min - ion o - ver all.

4. In your hand are power and might; it is yours to

give gran - deur and strength to all.

5. Therefore, our God, we give you thanks and we praise

the maj - es - ty of your name.

6. Glory to the Father, and to the Son, and to the Ho - ly Spir - it.

As in the beginning, so now and for ev - er. A - men!

Celebrant: Let us pray.

Pause for silent prayer.

God our Father, in Christ Jesus the faithful witness, you have made us a line of kings and priests to serve you. Teach us to praise you in gladness and simplicity of heart, that we may one day share the glorious kingdom of your Son, who lives and reigns with you in the unity of the Holy Spirit, one God, for ever and ever.

All: Amen.

STAND

PSALM 146—God loves the poor

English version:
David F. Wright, O.P.

S.M.

St. Thomas—A. Williams'
New Universal Psalmodist, 1770

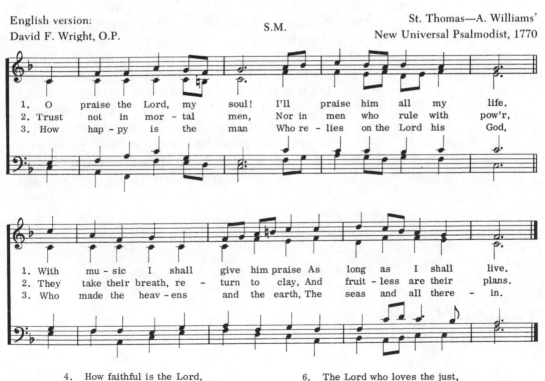

1. O praise the Lord, my soul! I'll praise him all my life.
2. Trust not in mor - tal men, Nor in men who rule with pow'r,
3. How hap - py is the man Who re - lies on the Lord his God,

1. With mu - sic I shall give him praise As long as I shall live.
2. They take their breath, re - turn to clay, And fruit - less are their plans.
3. Who made the heav - ens and the earth, The seas and all there - in.

4. How faithful is the Lord,
And just to the oppressed.
The hungry he supplies with bread;
The captive gains release.

5. The blind receive their sight,
He straightens those bowed low;
The stranger, widow, orphan too
In him shall be secure.

6. The Lord who loves the just,
Shall thwart the wicked man.
In power he for ever reigns,
Our God from age to age.

7. O praise the Lord, my soul!
The Father and the Son,
Who with the Spirit ever reign
While endless ages run.

Celebrant: Let us pray.

Pause for silent prayer.

Hear our prayers, Almighty Father, and keep us in your truth. Teach us compassion for the poor and defenseless that we may praise you sincerely, in and through Christ our Lord.

All: Amen.

III. Reading

SIT

A reading from the letter of blessed Paul the Apostle to the Colossians (3:16–17): Christ's peace must reign in your hearts, since as members of the one body you have been called to that peace. Dedicate yourselves to thankfulness. Let the word of Christ, rich as it is, dwell in you. In wisdom made perfect, instruct and admonish one another. Sing gratefully to God from your hearts in psalms, hymns, and inspired songs. Whatever you do, whether in speech or in action, do it in the name of the Lord Jesus. Give thanks to God the Father through him. This is the word of the Lord.

All: Thanks be to God.

A period of silent reflection or brief homily follow. On special days another reading may be added.

IV. Gospel Canticle

STAND

CANTICLE OF ZECHARIAH

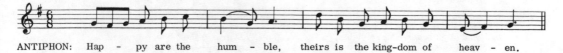

ANTIPHON: Hap - py are the   hum - ble,   theirs is the king-dom of   heav - en.

Verses of the Canticle: p.20; or the alternate setting may be used.

V. Intercessions

STAND: The ASSISTANT MINISTER/CANTOR sings the petitions, and the people sing the response after each petition.

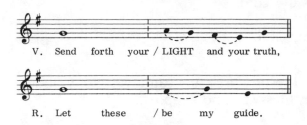

V. Send forth your / LIGHT and your truth,

R. Let these / be my guide.

V: In you is the/SOURCE OF life.

R: In your light we shall/SEE light.

V: Make us walk in your/truth and TEACH us.

R: For you are God our/SAVior.

V: Let your face shine/on your SERvants.

R: Save us/in your love.

V: Clothe your/priests in righteousness.

R: And make your chosen people/JOYful.

V: Lord, give your/PEOPLE strength.

R: Bless your peo/ple with peace.

Celebrant: Lord God almighty, the beginning and the end, the first and the last, direct our hearts and bodies in the love of God and the patience of Christ; bless us, defend us from all evil and bring us safely to life everlasting; through Jesus Christ our Lord.

All: Amen.

VI. Lord's Prayer

See p. 24

VII. Blessing and Dismissal

Assistant: Let us/bless the Lord.

All: Thanks be to/God.

Celebrant: May our Lord Jesus Christ, the same yesterday, today and for ever, bless/us and keep us.

All: A/men.

A sign of peace may be exchanged.

Monday—Evensong

I. Light Service

STAND

EVENING HYMN

James Quinn, S.J.
1969

84.84.88.84

Ar Hyd Y Nos
Welsh Traditional Melody

1. Day is done, but Love un-fail-ing Dwells ev-er here;
2. Dark des-cends, but Light un-end-ing Shines through our night;
3. Eyes will close, but you, un-sleep-ing, Watch by our side;

1. Shad-ows fall, but hope, pre-vail-ing, Calms ev'-ry fear.
2. You are with us, ev-er lead-ing New strength to sight;
3. Death may come: in Love's safe keep-ing Still we a-bide.

1. Lov-ing Fa-ther, none for-sak-ing, Take our hearts, of Love's own mak-ing,
2. One in love, your truth con-fess-ing, One in hope of heav-en's bless-ing,
3. God of love, all e-vil quell-ing, Sin for-giv-ing, fear dis-pell-ing,

1. Watch our sleep-ing, guard our wak-ing, Be al-ways near!
2. May we see, in love's pos-sess-ing, Love's end-less light!
3. Stay with us, our hearts in-dwell-ing, This ev-en-tide!

THANKSGIVING

Assistant: The Lord be with you.

All: And also with you.

Assistant: Blessed are you, O Lord our God, King of the universe, the Creator of light and darkness, the origin and preserver of all that exists. Remember your Church, O Holy Father, protect it from all evil, perfect it in your love, gather it from the four winds and bring it into your kingdom; for yours is the power and the glory, now and for ever.

All: Amen.

II. Psalmody

STAND: As Psalm 141 is sung, the CELEBRANT places incense in the thurible, and the ASSISTANT MINISTER incenses the candle, the celebrant, the other ministers, and the people.

PSALM 141—An evening prayer for forgiveness and protection.

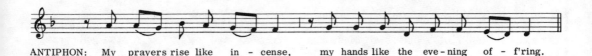

ANTIPHON: My prayers rise like in - cense, my hands like the eve - ning of - f'ring.

Psalm verses: p. 3. After the psalm is completed the celebrant begins the prayer immediately.

Celebrant: In your mercy hear our evening prayer, O God of compassion, that freed from the darkness of sin we may always walk in your light; through Jesus Christ our Lord.

All: Amen.

The people may sit or stand during the remaining psalmody; they stand, however, for the collects

PSALM 91

"I have given you power to tread on snakes and scorpions and all the forces of the enemy." (Luke 10:19)

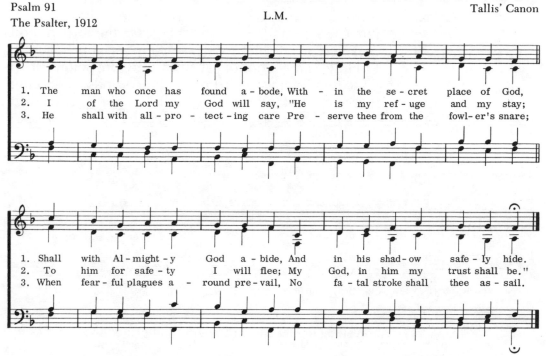

Psalm 91
The Psalter, 1912

L.M.

Tallis' Canon

1. The man who once has found a - bode, With - in the se - cret place of God,
2. I of the Lord my God will say, "He is my ref - uge and my stay;
3. He shall with all - pro - tect - ing care Pre - serve thee from the fowl - er's snare;

1. Shall with Al - might - y God a - bide, And in his shad - ow safe - ly hide.
2. To him for safe - ty I will flee; My God, in him my trust shall be."
3. When fear - ful plagues a - round pre - vail, No fa - tal stroke shall thee as - sail.

4. His out-spread pinions shall thee hide;
   Beneath his wings shalt thou confide;
   His faithfulness shall ever be
   A shield and buckler unto thee.

5. No nightly terrors shall alarm;
   No deadly shaft by day shall harm,
   Nor pestilence that walks by night,
   Nor plagues that waste in noon-day light.

6. Because thy trust is God alone,
   Thy dwelling place the Highest One,
   No evil shall upon thee come
   Nor plagues approach thy guarded home.

Celebrant: Let us pray.

Pause for silent prayer.

O God, the author of peace and lover of concord, to know you is to live, to serve you is to reign; defend us from all the assaults of our enemies, that we who trust in your protection may have no foe to fear; through the power of Jesus Christ our Lord.

All: Amen.

EPHESIANS 1:3–10—The Father's plan for holiness

English version: NAB   Frank Quinn, O.P.

CANTOR: Blest be God for ev - er: ALL: Let us bless his ho - ly name.
(or choir)

Blest be God for ev - er: ALL: Let us bless his ho - ly name.

1. Praised be the God and Father of our Lord Je - sus Christ,

who has bestowed on us in Christ every spiritual blessing in the heav - ens!

2. God chose us in him before the world be - gan,

to be holy and blameless in his sight, to be full of love;

3. He likewise predestined us through Christ Jesus to be his a - dop - ted sons

such was his will and plea - sure that all might praise the

glorious favor he has bestowed on us in his be - lov - ed.

4. It is in Christ and through his blood we have been redeemed and our sins for - giv - en,

so immeasurably generous is God's fa - vor to us.

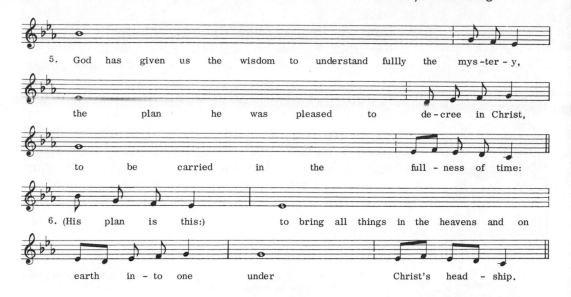

5. God has given us the wisdom to understand fullly the mys-ter-y,
the plan he was pleased to de-cree in Christ,
to be carried in the full-ness of time:
6. (His plan is this:) to bring all things in the heavens and on
earth in-to one under Christ's head-ship.

Celebrant: Let us pray.

Pause for silent prayer.

Almighty and everlasting God, who appointed your only-begotten Son the Savior of the world, and willed to accept the free gift of his blood for our redemption, grant that we may so venerate this price of our salvation that we may be defended on earth by its power from the evils of this present life and be made glad in heaven by its everlasting fruit; through the same Christ our Lord.

All: Amen.

III. Reading

SIT

A reading from the letter of blessed Paul the Apostle to the Ephesians (6:10–18): Draw your strength from the Lord and his mighty power. Put on the armor of God so that you may be able to stand firm against the tactics of the devil. Our battle is not against human forces but against the principalities and powers, the rulers of this world of darkness, the evil spirits in regions above. You must put on the armor of God if you are to resist on the evil day; do all that your duty requires, and hold your ground. Stand fast, with the truth as the belt around your waist, justice as your breastplate, and zeal to propagate the gospel of peace as your footgear. In all circumstances hold faith up before you as your shield; it will help you extinguish the fiery darts of the evil one. Take the helmet of salvation and the sword of the spirit, the word of God. At every opportunity pray in the Spirit, using prayers and petitions of every sort. Pray constantly and attentively for all in the holy company. This is the word of the Lord.

All: Thanks be to God.

A period of silent reflection or brief homily follow. On special days another reading may be added.

IV. Gospel Canticle

STAND

CANTICLE OF MARY

ANTIPHON: You have found fa - vor, Mar - y, in God's eyes.

Verses of the Canticle: p. 8. The alternate setting of the Canticle may be used, or one of the settings of the Canticle of Simeon.

V. Intercessions

STAND: The ASSISTANT MINISTER/CANTOR sings the petitions, and the people sing the response after each petition.

1. In peace, let us pray to the Lord.

R: Lord, have mercy.

2. For the peace, concord and stability of the whole world and for all churches, let us pray to the Lord.
3. For our country and every country and for the faithful dwelling in them, let us pray to the Lord.

4. For seasonable weather, for good harvests and for the prosperity of the whole world, let us pray to the Lord.

5. For lasting peace and a sinless life by day and by night, let us pray to the Lord.

6. For the union of charity, the bond of perfection, the gift of the Spirit, let us pray to the Lord.

7. For the forgiveness of sins, for all that enhances our human existence and pleases our God, let us pray to the Lord.

8. For the loving kindness of our merciful God and Father, let us pray to the Lord.

9. Help, save, pity and defend us, O God, by your grace. *(Pause)*

10. Rejoicing in the fellowship of the Blessed Virgin Mary, of St. *Name,* and of all the saints, let us commend ourselves, one another and our whole life to Christ our Lord.

R: To you, O Lord.

Celebrant: Father of mercies and God of all consolation, Creator and Preserver of all things, who are good by nature and the giver of all good things, save us all through your grace and increase in us your peace and tranquility and have mercy on us; through Jesus Christ our Lord.

All: Amen.

VI. Lord's Prayer

See p. 34

VII. Blessing and Dismissal

The ASSISTANT MINISTER sings:

Assistant: Bow down your heads to the Lord.

With raised hand the CELEBRANT imparts a blessing

Celebrant: May the God and Father of our Lord Jesus Christ bless you and keep/you.

All: Amen.

Celebrant: May the God of peace graciously smile/upon you.

All: Amen.

Celebrant: May the/Lord grant you peace.

All: Amen.

A sign of peace may be exchanged.

Tuesday—Morning Prayer

I. Invitatory

STAND

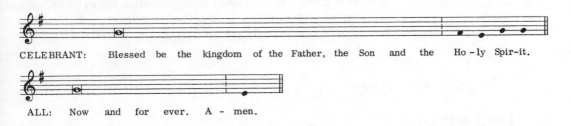

CELEBRANT: Blessed be the kingdom of the Father, the Son and the Ho-ly Spir-it.

ALL: Now and for ever. A - men.

MORNING HYMN

Psalm 100   Iste Confessor (Rouen)
James Quinn, S.J., 1969   11 11.11 5

1. Sing, all cre - a - tion, sing to God in glad - ness! Joy - ous - ly
2. Know that our God is Lord of all the a - ges! He is our
3. En - ter his tem - ple, ring - ing out his prais - es! Sing in thanks-

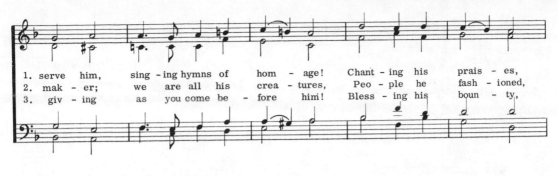

1. serve him,   sing-ing hymns of   hom - age!   Chant-ing his   prais - es,
2. mak - er;   we   are all his   crea - tures,   Peo - ple he   fash - ioned,
3. giv - ing   as   you come be - fore   him!   Bless-ing his   boun - ty,

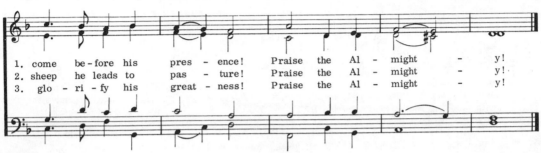

1. come   be - fore his   pres - ence!   Praise   the   Al - might - y!
2. sheep   he leads to   pas - ture!   Praise   the   Al - might - y!
3. glo - ri - fy his   great - ness!   Praise   the   Al - might - y!

4. Great in his goodness is the Lord we worship!
    Steadfast his kindness, love that knows no ending!
    Faithful his word is, changeless, everlasting!
    Praise the Almighty!

Celebrant: The Lord be with you.

All: And also with you.

The prayer follows immediately.

Celebrant: Lord Jesus Christ, Son of the living God and light of the world, in our morning worship give us strength for the coming day and power to glorify you and your holy Father and your life-giving Spirit, now and for ever.

All: Amen.

II. Psalmody

The people may sit during the first two psalms; they stand, however, for the collects and the Psalm of Praise.

PSALM 92—Song of those who are right with God

English version: Grail

Frank Quinn, O.P.

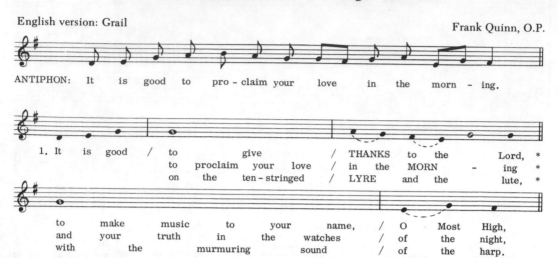

ANTIPHON: It is good to pro-claim your love in the morn - ing.

1. It is good / to give / THANKS to the Lord, *
   to proclaim your love / in the MORN – ing *
   on the ten-stringed / LYRE and the lute, *

   to make music to your name, / O Most High,
   and your truth in the watches / of the night,
   with the murmuring sound / of the harp.

2. Your deeds, O Lord, have / MADE ME glad; * for the work of your hands I / shout with joy.
   O Lord, how / GREAT are your works! * How deep are / your designs!
   The foolish man / cannot KNOW this * and the fool cannot / understand.

3. Though the wicked / SPRING up like grass * and all who do / evil thrive:
   they are doomed to be e / ternally destroyed. *
   But you, Lord, are eternal / ly on high.
   See how your / eneMIES perish; * all doers of evil are / SCATtered.

4. To me you give the / WILD - OX'S strength; * you anoint me with the / purest oil.
   My eyes looked in / triumph on my foes; * my ears heard gladly / of their fall.
   The just will / flourish like the palm - tree * and grow like a Lebanon / CEdar.

5. Planted in the / HOUSE of the Lord * they will flourish in the courts / of our God,
   still bearing fruit when / THEY ARE old, * still full of sap, / STILL green,
   to proclaim / that the Lord is just. * in him, my rock, there / is no wrong.
   Glory to the Father, and to the Son, and / to the Holy Spirit: *
   As in the beginning, so now and for ever / A - men.

Celebrant: Let us pray.

Pause for silent prayer.

Most High God, Rock of our salvation, we give you thanks for the coming of a new day in which we can celebrate your mighty deeds on our behalf; plant us deep in your designs and make us bear fruit for eternity; through Jesus Christ our Lord.

All: Amen.

ISAIAH 12:1–6—Christ, the source of the life-giving Spirit

English version: NAB

Frank Quinn, O.P.

ANTIPHON: From his heart flow foun-tains of liv - ing wa - ter.

1. I give you thanks, O Lord; though you have been an - gry with me,

your anger has abated and you have con - soled me.

2. God indeed is my sav - ior; I am confident and un - a - fraid.

My strength and courage is the Lord, and he has been my sav - ior.

3. With joy you will draw wa - ter at the fountain of sal - va - tion.

Give thanks to the Lord, ac - claim his name;

4. among the nations make known his deeds, proclaim how ex - alted is his name.

5. Sing praise to the Lord for his glo - rious a - chieve - ment;

let this be known through - out all the earth.

6. Shout with exultation, O cit - y of Zi - on,

for great in your midst is the Holy One of . Is - ra - el!

7. Glory to the Father, and to the Son, and to the Holy Spirit.

As in the beginning, so now and for ever. Amen!

Celebrant: Let us pray.

Pause for silent prayer.

Heavenly Father, from the pierced side of Christ came blood and water as indelible signs of love made visible and of the outpouring of the Spirit which those who believed in him were to receive. May the fountains of living water which flow from the heart of Jesus quench the thirst of those who seek you with all their hearts; through the same Jesus Christ our Lord.

All: Amen.

STAND

PSALM 147A—Praise the providence of God

Psalm 147
The Psalter, 1912, alt.

76.76.D

St. Theodulph
Melchior Teschner, pub. 1615

1. Come, sing your al - le - lu - ias! 'Tis good our God to praise;
2. The star - ry hosts he num - bers, He calls them all by name;
3. The heav'ns with clouds he cov - ers, He sends the cheer - ing rain;

1. 'Tis pleas-ant and be - com - ing To him our songs to raise;
2. His great-ness and his wis - dom His won - drous works pro - claim;
3. The slopes of all the moun - tains He fills with grass and grain;

1. He builds the walls of Zi - on, He seeks her wand'-ring sons,
2. The meek he lifts to hon - or, He hum - bles sin - ful pride;
3. To beast and bird his good - ness Their dai - ly food sup - plies;

1. He binds their wounds and com - forts The bro - ken - heart - ed ones.
2. Give thanks to him and ut - ter His prais - es far and wide.
3. He cares for all his crea - tures, At - ten - tive to their cries.

4. No human pow'r delights him,
   No earthly pomp or pride;
   He loves the meek who fear him
   And in his love confide;
   All praise to God the Father,
   To God the son be praise,
   And to the Holy Spirit
   Our joyful voices raise.

Celebrant: Let us pray.

Pause for silent prayer.

Good Father, our consoler and our comforter, lift up the humble and cast down the proud, put an end to our sinning, establish harmony in our lives and bring us home to you, the Author of life; through Jesus Christ our Lord.

All: Amen.

III. Reading

SIT

A reading from the letter of blessed Paul the Apostle to the Romans (1:2–6): This is the gospel of God which he promised long ago through his prophets, as the holy Scriptures record—the gospel concerning his Son, who was descended from David according to the flesh but was made Son of God in power according to the spirit of holiness, by his resurrection from the dead: Jesus Christ our Lord. Through him we have been favored with apostleship, that we may spread his name and bring to obedient faith all the Gentiles, among whom are you who have been called to belong to Jesus Christ. This is the word of the Lord.

All: Thanks be to God.

A period of silent reflection or brief homily follow. On special days another reading may be added.

IV. Gospel Canticle

STAND

CANTICLE OF ZECHARIAH

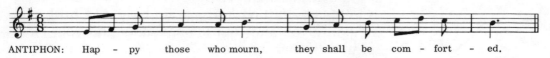

ANTIPHON: Hap - py   those   who mourn,   they shall   be   com - fort - ed.

Verses of the Canticle: p. 20; or the alternate setting may be used.

V. Intercessions

STAND: The ASSISTANT MINISTER/CANTOR sings the petitions, and the people sing the response after each petition.

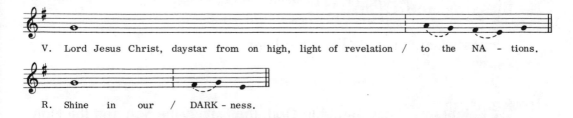

V. Lord Jesus Christ, daystar from on high, light of revelation / to the NA - tions.

R. Shine   in   our / DARK - ness.

V: Lord Jesus Christ, light up the world with the sunshine of your/SAVING word.

R: Shine in our/DARKness.

V: Lord Jesus Christ, renew us in the image and/LIKEness of God.

R: Shine in our/DARKness.

V: Lord Jesus Christ, teach us to praise you in/THOUGHT, word and deed.

R: Shine in our/DARKness.

V: Lord Jesus Christ, keep us today from/ALL sin and danger.

R: Shine in our/DARKness.

Other petitions may be added

Celebrant: Only-begotten Son and Word of God, for our salvation you took flesh of the Blessed Virgin Mary and became man; you were crucified and trampled down death by your death and rose again on the third day; forgive us our sins, sanctify us to your service and bring us to life everlasting: for you are holy, O Christ, and we glorify you and your loving Father and your Holy Spirit, now and for ever.

All: Amen.

VI. Lord's Prayer

See p. 24

VII. Blessing and Dismissal

Assistant: Let us/bless the Lord.

All: Thanks be to/God.

Celebrant: May almighty God, the Father, the Son and the Holy Spirit, bless/us and keep us.

All: A/men.

A sign of peace may be exchanged.

Tuesday—Evensong

I. Light Service

STAND

CELEBRANT: Je - sus Christ is the light of the world.

ALL: A light no dark - ness can ex - tin - guish.

EVENING HYMN

Christe qui Lux es et Dies, c. 800
Tr. & adap. Rev. M. Quinn, O.P. et al

C.M.

St. Anne
William Croft, 1708

1. O Christ, you are the light and day Which drives a - way the night,
2. As now the ev' - ning shad - ows fall Please grant us, Lord, we pray,
3. Re - mem - ber us, poor mor - tal men, We hum - bly ask, O Lord,

1. The ev - er shin - ing Sun of God And pledge of fu - ture light.
2. A qui - et night to rest in you Un - til the break of day.
3. And may your pres - ence in our souls, Be now our great re - ward.

THANKSGIVING

Assistant: The Lord be with you

All: And also with you.

Assistant: Blessed are you, O Lord our God, King of the universe, for your goodness and loving-kindness to us and to all men. We praise you for our making, for our preservation and for all the blessings of this day. Above all we praise you for saving the world through Jesus Christ our Lord—for the means of grace and for the hope of glory. Grant us such awareness of your mercies that with truly thankful hearts we may praise you, not only with our lips, but with our lives, by dedicating ourselves to your service in holiness and righteousness all our days; all honor and praise to the Father and the Holy Spirit through Jesus Christ our Lord, now and for ever.

All: Amen.

II. Psalmody

STAND: As Psalm 141 is sung, the CELEBRANT places incense in the thurible, and the ASSISTANT MINISTER incenses the candle, the celebrant, the other ministers, and the people.

PSALM 141—An evening prayer for forgiveness and protection

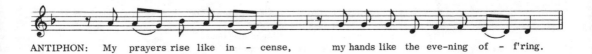

ANTIPHON: My prayers rise like in - cense, my hands like the eve-ning of - f'ring.

Psalm verses: p. 3. After the psalm is completed the celebrant begins the prayer immediately.

Celebrant: Let the incense of our repentant prayer ascend before you, O Lord, and let your loving kindness descend upon us, that with purified minds we may sing your praises with the whole heavenly host and glorify you for ever and ever.

All: Amen.

The people may sit or stand during the remaining psalmody; they stand, however, for the collects.

PSALM 113
"Blest are the lowly; they shall inherit the earth." (Mt 5:5)

Psalm 113
The Psalter, 1912, alt.

L.M.

Eisenach
From a melody by
J. H. Shein, 1586–1630

1. Praise God, you serv-ants of the Lord, O praise his name with one ac-cord;
2. From ris-ing un-to set-ting sun Praised be the Lord, the Might-y One;
3. On whom but God can we re-ly The Lord our God who reigns on high,

1. O bless the Lord, his name a-dore From this time forth for ev-er-more.
2. He reigns o'er all su-preme in might, A-bove the heav'ns in glo-ry bright.
3. Who con-des-cends to see and know The things of heav'n and earth be-low.

4. He lifts the poor and makes them great,
   With joy he fills the desolate;
   O praise the Lord and bless his name,
   His mercy and his might proclaim.

Celebrant: Let us pray.

Pause for silent prayer.

Look down, O Lord, from your heavenly throne,
illuminate the darkness of this coming night with your
celestial brightness and from the sons of light banish
the deeds of darkness; through Jesus Christ our Lord.

All: Amen.

REVELATION 4:11; 5:9,10,12—All heaven worships the Lamb

English version: NAB

Frank Quinn, O.P.

ANTIPHON: To the Lamb be glo - ry, hon - or and power.

ANTIPHON harmony: To the Lamb be glo - ry, hon - or and power.

1a. O Lord our God, you are wor - thy to re - ceive glo - ry and hon - or and power!

1b. For you have cre-a-ted all things; by your will they came to be and were made!

2a. Wor-thy are you to re - ceive the scroll and break o - pen its seals, for you were slain.

2b. With your blood you pur - chased for God men of ev - er - y race

and tongue, of ev - ery peo - ple and na - tion.

3a. You made of them a king-dom, and priests to serve our God, and they shall reign on the earth.

3b. Wor - thy is the Lamb that was slain to re - ceive power and rich - es,

wis - dom and strength, hon - or and glo - ry and praise!

4a. Glo - ry to the Fa - ther, and to the Son, and to the Ho - ly Spir - it.

4b. As in the be - gin - ning, so now and for ev - er. A - men.

Celebrant: Let us pray.

Pause for silent prayer.

O God of peace, who brought our Lord Jesus back from the dead to become the great Shepherd of the sheep by the blood that sealed an eternal covenant, make us ready to do your will in every kind of good action and turn us into whatever is acceptable to you; through the same Jesus Christ, to whom be glory for ever and ever.

All: Amen.

III. Reading

SIT

A reading from the letter of blessed Paul the Apostle to the Romans (3:21–26): Now the justice of God has been manifested apart from the law, even though both law and prophets bear witness to it—that justice of God which works through faith in Jesus Christ for all who believe. All men have sinned and are deprived of the glory of God. All men are now undeservedly justified by the gift of God, through the redemption wrought in Christ Jesus. Through his blood, God made him the means of expiation for all who believe. He did so to manifest his own justice, for the sake of remitting sins committed in the past—to manifest his justice in the present, by way of forbearance, so that he might be just and might justify those who believe in Jesus. This is the word of the Lord.

All: Thanks be to God.

A period of silent reflection or brief homily follow. On special days another reading may be added.

IV. Gospel Canticle

STAND

CANTICLE OF MARY

ANTIPHON: The Lord has done mar-vels for me, Ho - ly is his name.

Verses of the Canticle: p. 8. The alternate setting of the Canticle may be used, or one of the settings of the Canticle of Simeon.

V. Intercessions

STAND: The ASSISTANT MINISTER/CANTOR sings the petitions, and the people sing the response after each petition.

1. In peace let us pray to the Lord.

R: Lord have mercy.

2. For the Holy Church of God that it bear faithful witness to the Good News of the Gospel, let us pray to the Lord.

3. For our holy father, *Name,* that he be established in health and wisdom for the sake of the Universal Church, let us pray to the Lord.

4. For our bishop, *Name,* that he may stand and feed his flock to the glory of God's holy Name, let us pray to the Lord,

5. For those in holy orders, for our missionaries, for monks and nuns and all religious, that they be truly dedicated to their special callings, let us pray to the Lord.

6. For the heads of governments, that their minds and hearts be directed by God's will for our lasting peace, let us pray to the Lord.

7. For the sick and the dying, the hungry and the imprisoned, the persecuted and the afflicted, that they may rejoice in divine assistance in their hour of need, let us pray to the Lord.

8. For our friends, relatives and benefactors, that they may experience God's providential care, let us pray to the Lord.

9. For the conversion of sinners, the reconciliation of separated Christians, and the enlightenment of unbelievers, let us pray to the Lord.

10. For the faithful departed that they may enjoy

refreshment, light and peace, let us pray to the Lord.
11. Help, save, pity and defend us, O God, by your grace. *(Pause)*
12. Rejoicing in the fellowship of the Blessed Virgin Mary, of St. *Name,* and of all the saints, let us commend ourselves, one another and our whole life to Christ our Lord.

R: To you, O Lord.

Celebrant: Heavenly Father, Lord of the living and of the dead, we pray that those for whom we intercede, whether still detained in this life or already living in the next, may obtain from your loving kindness the remission of their sins and all that is helpful toward salvation; through Jesus Christ our Lord.

All: Amen.

VI. Lord's Prayer

See p. 34

VII. Blessing and Dismissal

The ASSISTANT MINISTER sings:

Assistant: Bow down your heads to the Lord.

With raised hand the CELEBRANT imparts a blessing.

Celebrant: May the Lord bless you and keep/you.

All: Amen.

Celebrant: May the Lord graciously smile/upon you.

All: Amen.

Celebrant: May the/Lord grant you peace.

All: Amen.

A sign of peace may be exchanged.

Wednesday—Morning Prayer

I. Invitatory

STAND

CELEBRANT: Glory to God in the high-est.

ALL: Peace to his people on earth.

MORNING HYMN

Psalm 95
James Quinn, S.J., 1969

66.66.44.44

Darwall's 148th
John Darwall, 1731-89

1. To God with glad-ness sing, Your Rock and Sav-ior bless; With-
2. He crad-les in his hand The heights and depths of earth; He
3. Your heav'n-ly Fa-ther praise, Ac-claim his on-ly Son, Your

1. in his tem-ple bring Your songs of thank-ful-ness! O God of
2. made the sea and land, He brought the world to birth! O God most
3. voice in hom-age raise To him who makes all one! O Dove of

1. might, To you we sing, En-throned as King On heav-en's height!
2. high, We are your sheep; On us you keep Your Shep-herd's eye!
3. peace, On us des-cend That strife may end And joy in-crease!

Celebrant: The Lord be with you.

All: And also with you.

The prayer follows immediately.

Celebrant: Lord Jesus Christ, light of the world and teacher of righteousness, teach us to enter by the narrow gate that leads to life and to do always the will of your Father who is in heaven, O Savior of the world, who live and reign for ever and ever.

All: Amen.

II. Psalmody

The people may sit during the first two psalms; they stand, however, for the collects and the Psalm of Praise.

PSALM 43—Longing for our heavenly home

English version: Grail   Frank Quinn, O.P.

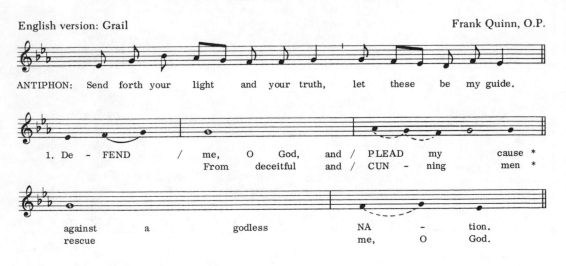

ANTIPHON: Send forth your light and your truth, let these be my guide.

1. De - FEND / me, O God, and / PLEAD my cause *
   From deceitful and / CUN - ning men *

   against a godless NA - tion.
   rescue me, O God.

2.   Since you, O God, are / my STRONGhold, * why have you re / jected me?
     Why do / I go mourning * oppressed / by the foe?

3.   O send forth your / light and your truth; * let these be / MY guide.
     Let them bring me to your / HOly mountain * to the place where / YOU dwell.

4.   And I will come to the / altar of God, * the God / of my joy.
     My redeemer, I will thank / you on the harp, * O / God, my God.

5. Why are you / cast down, my soul, * why groan with / IN me?
    Hope in God; I will / PRAISE him still, * my savior / and my God.

6. Glory to the Father, and to the Son, and to the / HOly Spirit: *
    As in the beginning, so now and for ever. / A - men.

Celebrant: Let us pray.

Pause for silent prayer.

My Savior and the God of my joy, send forth your
light and your truth, rescue us from the godless and
help us to praise you as you deserve; for you are
merciful and you love mankind, Father, Son and Holy
Spirit, now and for ever.

All: Amen.

CANTICLE OF HANNAH—Christ is the exaltation of the poor and the peaceable (1 Samuel 2: 1–10)

English version: NAB   Frank Quinn, O.P.

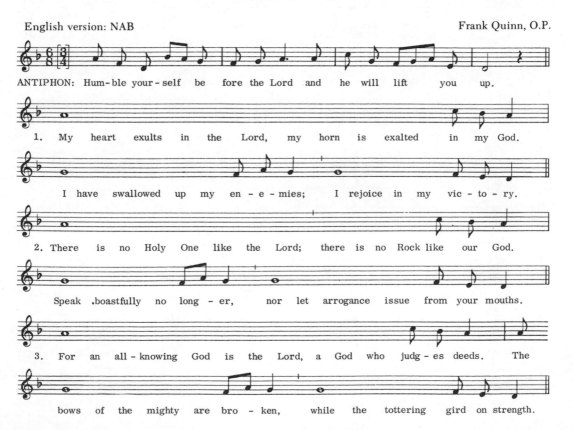

ANTIPHON: Hum-ble your-self be fore the Lord and he will lift you up.

1. My heart exults in the Lord, my horn is exalted in my God.
    I have swallowed up my en-e-mies; I rejoice in my vic-to-ry.

2. There is no Holy One like the Lord; there is no Rock like our God.
    Speak .boastfully no long-er, nor let arrogance issue from your mouths.

3. For an all-knowing God is the Lord, a God who judg-es deeds. The
    bows of the mighty are bro-ken, while the tottering gird on strength.

4. The well-fed hire themselves out for bread, while the hungry bat-ten on spoil.

The barren wife bears sev-en sons, while the mother of many lan-guish-es.

5. The Lord puts to death and gives life; he casts down to the nether world; he raises up a-gain.

The Lord makes poor and makes rich, he humbles, he al-so ex-alts.

6. He raises the needy from the dust; from the ash heap he liffts up the poor,

To seat them with nobles and make a glorious throne their her-i-tage.

He gives to the vower his vow, and blesses the sleep of the just.

7. For the pillars of the earth are the Lord's, and he has set the world

up-on them. He will guard the footsteps of his

faith-ful ones, but the wicked shall perish in the dark-ness.

8. For not by strength does man prevail; the Lord's foes shall be shat-tered.

The Most High in heaven thun-ders; the Lord judges the ends of the earth.

9. Now may he give strength to his king, and exalt the horn of his a-noint-ed!

Glory to the Father, and to the Son, and to the Holy Spir-it.

As in the beginning, so now and for ever. A - men!

Celebrant: Let us pray.

Pause for silent prayer.

Lord of life and of death, who raised our Savior Jesus Christ from the grave and exalted him to a glorious throne at your right hand, lift up the poor and lowly who put their trust in you as did the prophetess Hannah and the Blessed Virgin Mary, the chosen mother of the same Jesus Christ our Lord, who lives and reigns with you in the unity of the Holy Spirit, one God, now and for ever.

All. Amen.

STAND

PSALM 147B—God's personal care for his chosen.

Psalm 147
The Psalter, 1912, alt.

76.76.D.

Bremen—Melody adap. from
Storl's *Wurtemberg Gesangbuch*, 1710

1. O praise your God, O Zi - on, His gra - cious aid con - fess;
2. A - gain he gives com - mand - ment; The winds of sum - mer blow,
3. For match - less grace and mer - cy Your grate - ful prais - es bring;

1. He gives you peace and plen - ty, His gifts your chil - dren bless.
2. The snow and ice are melt - ed, A - gain the wa - ters flow.
3. To him give thanks for - ev - er, And al - le - lu - ias sing.

1. He sends his swift com - mand - ment, And snow and ice en - fold
2. His stat - utes and his judg - ments He makes his peo - ple know;
3. All praise to God the Fa - ther, To God the Son be praise,

1. The world, and none are a - ble To stand be - fore his cold.
2. To them as to no oth - ers His grace he loves to show.
3. And to the Ho - ly Spir - it Our joy - ful voic - es raise.

Celebrant: Let us pray.

Pause for silent prayer.

Gracious Father, strengthen your church that the gates of hell may not prevail against it; establish us in peace and security and nourish us with your revealing word; through Jesus Christ our Lord.

All: Amen.

III. Reading

SIT

A reading from the letter of blessed Paul the Apostle to the Romans (8:14–17): All who are led by the Spirit of God are sons of God. You did not receive a spirit of slavery leading you back into fear, but a spirit of adoption through which we cry out, "Abba!" (that is, "Father"). The Spirit himself gives witness with our spirit that we are children of God. But if we are children, we are heirs as well: heirs of God, heirs with Christ, if only we suffer with him so as to be glorified with him. This is the word of the Lord.

All: Thanks be to God.

A period of silent reflection or brief homily follow. On special days another reading may be added.

IV. Gospel Canticle

STAND

CANTICLE OF ZECHARIAH

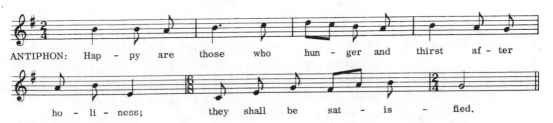

Verses of the canticle: p. 20; or the alternate setting may be used.

V. Intercessions

STAND: The ASSISTANT MINISTER/CANTOR sings the petitions, and the people sing the response after each petition.

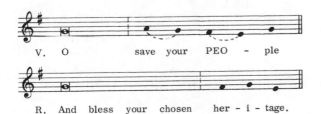

V: Nourish and/keep them by your power.

R: And lift them up for/Ever.

V: Day by day we/give you GLOry.

R: We revere your name e/ternally.

V: Give peace in our/TIME, O Lord.

R: Only you make us/rest secure.

V: Guard us this day from all/sin and DANger.

R: Have mercy, Lord, have/MERcy.

V: O Lord, let your mercy de/scend upON us.

R: For in/you we trust.

V: Hear our/PRAYERS, O Lord.

R: And let our cry/come to you.

Celebrant: Lord God, King of heaven and earth, direct and sanctify, rule and guide our hearts and bodies, our thoughts, words and deeds, to do your law and keep your commandments, so that today and every day we may be kept safe and free, O Savior of the world, who live and reign for ever and ever.

All: Amen.

VI. Lord's Prayer

See p. 24

VII. Blessing and Dismissal

Assistant: Let us/bless the Lord.

All: Thanks be to/God.

Celebrant: May the divine assistance of the Father, the Son and the Holy Spirit be/with us always.

All: A/men.

A sign of peace may be exchanged.

Wednesday—Evensong

I. Light Service

STAND

ASSISTANT: Je - sus Christ is the light of the world.

ALL: A light no dark-ness can ex-tin-guish.

EVENING HYMN

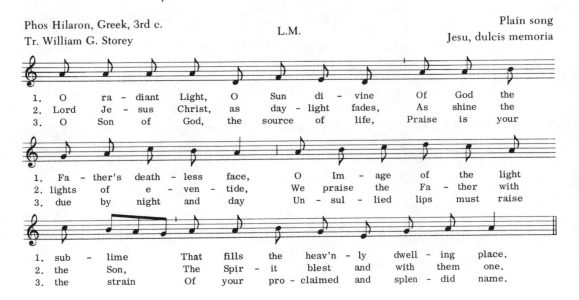

Phos Hilaron, Greek, 3rd c.
Tr. William G. Storey

L.M.

Plain song
Jesu, dulcis memoria

1. O ra - diant Light, O Sun di - vine Of God the
2. Lord Je - sus Christ, as day - light fades, As shine the
3. O Son of God, the source of life, Praise is your

1. Fa - ther's death - less face, O Im - age of the light
2. lights of e - ven - tide, We praise the Fa - ther with
3. due by night and day Un - sul - lied lips must raise

1. sub - lime That fills the heav'n - ly dwell - ing place.
2. the Son, The Spir - it blest and with them one.
3. the strain Of your pro - claimed and splen - did name.

THANKSGIVING

Assistant: The Lord be with you.

All: And also with you.

Assistant: Blessed are you, O Lord our God, King of the universe, who conducted our fathers in the faith by a pillar of cloud by day and a pillar of fire by night; light up our darkness by the light of your Christ; may his word be a lamp to our feet and a light to our path; for you are merciful and you love mankind, and we glorify you, Father, Son and Holy Spirit, now and for ever.

All: Amen.

II. Psalmody

STAND: As Psalm 141 is sung, the CELEBRANT places incense in the thurible, and the ASSISTANT MINISTER incenses the candle, the celebrant, the other ministers, and the people.

PSALM 141—An evening prayer for forgiveness and protection

ANTIPHON: My prayers rise like in - cense, my hands like the eve-ning of - f'ring.

Psalm verses: p. 3. After the psalm is completed the celebrant begins the prayer immediately.

Celebrant: Expell all darkness from our hearts, O Lord, and pour your light into our minds, through Jesus Christ our Lord.

All: Amen.

The people may sit or stand during the remaining psalmody; they stand, however, for the collects.

PSALM 90
"Christ sustains all things by his powerful word." (Heb 1:3)

Isaac Watts, 1674-1748

C.M.

St. Anne
William Croft, 1678-1727

1. O   God, our help in   a - ges past, Our   hope for years to   come,
2. Un - der the shad - ow   of   thy throne Still   may we dwell se - cure;
3. Be - fore the hills in   or - der stood, Or   earth re - ceived her   frame,

1. Our shel - ter from the storm - y blast, And our e - ter - nal home!
2. Suf - fi - cient is thine arm a - lone, And our de - fense is sure.
3. From ev - er - last - ing thou art God, To end - less years the same.

4. A thousand ages, in thy sight,
   Are like an ev'ning gone;
   Short as the watch that ends the night,
   Before the rising sun.

5. Time, like an ever rolling stream,
   Bears all its sons away;
   They fly forgotten, as a dream
   Dies at the opening day.

6. O God, our help in ages past,
   Our hope for years to come;
   Be thou our guide while life shall last,
   And our eternal home!

Celebrant: Let us pray.

Pause for silent prayer.

Hear our prayers, O Lord, and protect us both by night and by day, that whatever the changes and chances of this mortal life we may always find strength in your unchanging love; through Jesus Christ our Lord.

All: Amen.

COLOSSIANS 1:12–20—Christ reconciles God and man

English version: NAB   Frank Quinn, O.P.

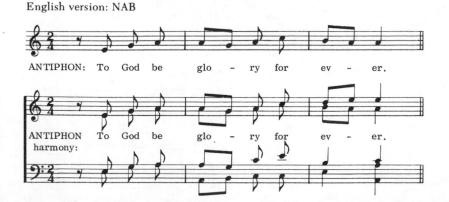

ANTIPHON: To God be glo - ry for ev - er.

ANTIPHON To God be glo - ry for ev - er.
harmony:

1. Let us give thanks to the Fa - ther for hav - ing made us wor - thy

to share the lot of the saints in light.

2. He res - cued us from the power of dark - ness

and brought us in - to the king - dom of his be - lov - ed Son.

Through him we have re - demp - tion, the for - give-ness of our sins.

3. He is the im - age of the In - vis - i ble God, the first - born

of all crea - tures. In him ev - er - y - thing in heav - en and on earth

was cre - a - ted, things vis - i - ble and in - vis - i - ble.

4. All (things) were cre - a - ted through him and for him. He is be - fore

all else that is. In him ev - er - y - thing con - tin - ues in be - ing.

5. It is he who is head of the bod - y, the church;

he who is the be - gin - ning, the first - born of the dead,

so that pri - ma - cy may be his in ev - 'ry - thing.

6. It pleased God to make ab - so - lute full - ness re - side in him and,

by means of him, to re-con-cile every-thing in his per-son, both on earth and in the heav-ens, mak-ing peace through the blood of his cross.

Celebrant: Let us pray.

Pause for silent prayer.

O God, our protector, look on the face of your Christ who delivered himself up to redeem mankind. Enable all men everywhere to glorify your name from sunrise to sunset and to offer you an unblemished sacrifice of praise; through the same Jesus Christ our Lord.

All: Amen.

III. Reading

SIT

A reading from the letter of blessed Paul the Apostle to the Romans (8:28–38): We know that God makes all things work together for the good of those who have been called according to his decree. Those whom he foreknew he predestined to share the image of his Son, that the Son might be the first-born of many brothers. Those he predestined he likewise called; those he called he also justified; and those he justified he in turn glorified. What shall we say after that? Is it possible that he who did not spare his own Son but handed him over for the sake of us all will not grant us all things besides? Who shall bring a charge against God's chosen ones? God, who justifies? Who shall condemn them? Christ Jesus, who died or rather was raised up, who is at the right hand of God and who intercedes for us? . . . I am certain that neither death nor life, neither angels nor principalities, neither the present nor the future, nor powers, neither height nor depth nor any other creature, will be able to separate us from the love of God that comes to us in Christ Jesus, our Lord. This is the word of the Lord.

All: Thanks be to God.

A period of silent reflection or brief homily follow. On special days another reading may be added.

IV. Gospel Canticle

STAND

CANTICLE OF MARY

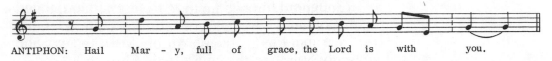

ANTIPHON: Hail Mar - y, full of grace, the Lord is with you.

Verses of the Canticle: p. 8. The alternate setting of the Canticle may be used, or one of the settings of the Canticle of Simeon.

V. Intercessions

STAND: The ASSISTANT MINISTER/CANTOR sings the petitions, and the people sing the response after each petition.

1. In peace, let us pray to the Lord.

R: Lord, have mercy.

2. For an evening that is perfect, holy, peaceful and without sin, let us pray to the Lord.

3. For an angel of peace, a faithful guide and guardian of our souls and bodies, let us pray to the Lord.

4. For the pardon and forgiveness of our sins and offenses, let us pray to the Lord.

5. For all that is good and profitable to our souls and for the peace of the world, let us pray to the Lord.

6. For peace and repentance for sin throughout the rest of our lives, let us pray to the Lord.

7. For a peaceful and Christian end to our lives, without shame or pain, and for a good defense before the awesome judgment seat of Christ, let us pray to the Lord.

8. Help, save, pity and defend us, O God, by your grace. *(Pause)*

9. Rejoicing in the fellowship of the Blessed Virgin Mary, of St. *Name,* and of all the saints, let us commend ourselves, one another and our whole life to Christ our Lord.

R: To you, O Lord.

Celebrant: O Lord our God, Creator and Redeemer of the human race, it is not from men but from you that we expect help and hope for salvation. Protect us this evening and throughout the night and at all times from danger, temptation and sin, for you are merciful, O God, and love mankind, and we glorify you, Father, Son and Holy Spirit, now and for ever.

All: Amen.

VI. Lord's Prayer

See p. 34

VII. Blessing and Dismissal

The ASSISTANT MINISTER sings:

Assistant: Bow down your heads to the Lord.

With raised hand the CELEBRANT imparts a blessing.

Celebrant: May Jesus Christ, the friend of mankind, bless you and keep/you.

All: Amen.

Celebrant: May the Son of God graciously smile/upon you.

All: Amen.

Celebrant: May the/Lord grant you peace.

All: Amen.

A sign of peace may be exchanged

Thursday—Morning Prayer

I. Invitatory

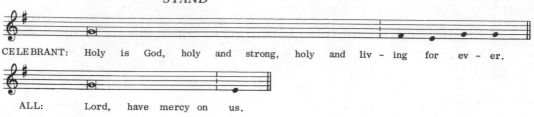

STAND

CELEBRANT: Holy is God, holy and strong, holy and liv-ing for ev-er.

ALL: Lord, have mercy on us.

MORNING HYMN

Psalm 95
The Psalter, 1912, alt.

C.M.

St. Peter
A. R. Reinagle, 1799-1877

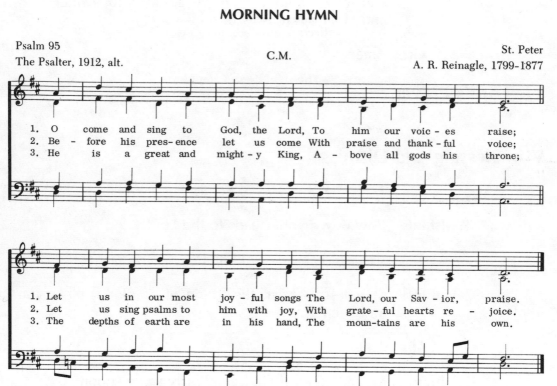

1. O come and sing to God, the Lord, To him our voic-es raise;
2. Be-fore his pres-ence let us come With praise and thank-ful voice;
3. He is a great and might-y King, A-bove all gods his throne;

1. Let us in our most joy-ful songs The Lord, our Sav-ior, praise.
2. Let us sing psalms to him with joy, With grate-ful hearts re-joice.
3. The depths of earth are in his hand, The moun-tains are his own.

4. To him the spacious sea belongs,
He made its waves and tides;
And by his hand the rising land
Was formed, and still abides.

5. O come, and bowing down to him
Our worship let us bring;
Yes, let us kneel before the Lord,
Our Maker and our King.

Celebrant: The Lord be with you.

All: And also with you.

The prayer follows immediately.

Celebrant: Lord Jesus Christ, crowned with glory and splendor, with light for your mantle, make our first concern the kingdom of God and what he requires of us and bring us in safety and joy to our heavenly home, O Savior of the world, who live and reign for ever and ever.

All: Amen.

II. Psalmody

The people may sit during the first two psalms; they stand, however, for the collects and the Psalm of Praise.

PSALM 57—The dawning of new hope

English version: Grail   Frank Quinn, O.P.

ANTIPHON: O God, a rise a-bove the heav-ens; may your glo-ry shine on earth.

1. Have MER - / cy   on   me,   / +   / GOD, have
   In the shadow of your wings   / I TAKE

   mer - cy * for in you my soul / has tak-en re - fuge.
   re - fuge * till the storms of de - struc-tion pass by.

2. I call to God / the MOST High, * to God who / has always been my help.
   May he send from heaven and save / me + and shame those who / asSAIL me. *
   May God send his / TRUTH and his love.

3. My soul lies / down among lions, * who would de / VOUR the sons of men.
   Their teeth are / SPEARS and arrows, * their / TONGUE a sharpened sword.
   O God, arise a / BOVE the heavens; * may / your glory shine on earth!

4. They laid a / snare for my steps, * my / SOUL was bowed down.
   They dug a / pit in my path * but fell / in it THEMselves.

5. My heart is ready, O / God, + my / HEART is ready. * I will sing / I will sing your praise.
    Awake my / soul, + awake / LYRE and harp, * I will / aWAKE the dawn.

6. I will thank you Lord a / MONG the peoples, * among the na / tions I will praise you.
    for your love reach / es to the heavens * and your / TRUTH to the skies.

7. O God, arise / above the heavens; * may your glo / ry SHINE on earth!
    Glory to the Father, and to the Son, and to the / HOly Spirit: *
    As in the beginning, so now and for / ever. A - men.

Celebrant: Let us pray.

Pause for silent prayer.

O God, our helper and our glory, give us unshakeable faith, firm hope and sincere love; bless our comings and our goings, our deeds and our desires, our work and our prayer and keep us in the shadow of your wings today and every day; through Jesus Christ our Lord.

All: Amen.

CANTICLE OF THE THREE YOUNG MEN—

Praise God, our Creator and our Redeemer, for ever (Daniel 3: 52–56)

English version: NAB   Frank Quinn, O.P.

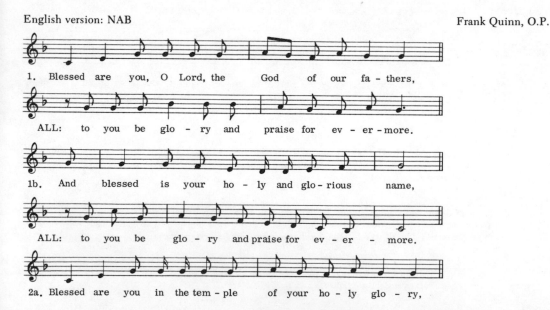

1. Blessed are you, O Lord, the God of our fa - thers,

ALL: to you be glo - ry and praise for ev - er - more.

1b. And blessed is your ho - ly and glo - rious name,

ALL: to you be glo - ry and praise for ev - er - more.

2a. Blessed are you in the tem - ple of your ho - ly glo - ry,

ALL: to you be glo - ry and praise for ev - er - more.

2b. Blessed are you on the throne of your king - dom,

ALL: to you be glo - ry and praise for ev - er - more.

3a. Blessed are you who look in - to the depths,

ALL: to you be glo - ry and praise for ev - er - more,

3b. from your throne up - on the cher - u - bim,

ALL: to you be glo - ry and praise for ev - er - more.

4a. Blessed are you in the fir - ma - ment of heav - en,

ALL: to you be glo - ry and praise for ev - er - more.

4b. Bless the Fa - ther, the Son, and Ho - ly Spir - it,

ALL: to you be glo - ry and praise for ev - er - more.

Celebrant: Let us pray.

Pause for silent prayer.

Lord Jesus Christ, by your death and resurrection you reconciled everything in heaven and on earth; by the power of your passion, set us apart to sing the praise of God in union with all the saints and angels, now and for ever.

All: Amen.

STAND

PSALM 148—A cosmic hymn of praise

St. 1,3: Foundling Hospital Collection,
c. 1801, alt: 87.87.D
St. 2: The Psalter, 1912, alt.

Hyfrydol
R. H. Prichard, 1811–87

1. Praise, the Lord, O heav'ns, a – dore him; Praise him, an – gels in the heights; Sun and moon, re – joice be – fore him; Praise him, shin – ing stars of light. Praise the Lord, for he has spo – ken; Worlds his
2. All cre – a – tion bow be – fore him; Seas and all that they con – tain, Storm – y winds that do his pleas – ure, Hail and light – ing, snow and rain. Hills and moun – tains, praise your Mak – er, Praise him,
3. All you na – tions, come be – fore him; Earth – ly ru – lers, all you kings; Young and old your praise ex – press – ing, Join – ing all cre – a – ted things. Praise the God of our sal – va – tion, Hosts on

1. might - y voice o - beyed; Laws which nev - er
2. all you flocks and herds, Fields and or - chards,
3. high, his pow'r pro - claim, Heav'n and earth and

1. shall be bro - ken, For their guid - ance he has made.
2. sing his glo - ry, Creep - ing things and fly - ing birds.
3. all cre - a - tion, Praise and mag - ni - fy his name.

Celebrant: Let us pray.

Pause for silent prayer.

We acknowledge that we are the work of your hands, O God our Father; may we not be silent in the face of your splendor but unite with all creatures, seen and unseen, in hymning your praise; through Jesus Christ our Lord.

All: Amen.

III. Reading

SIT

A reading from the letter of blessed Paul the Apostle to the Romans (12:1–2): I beg you through the mercy of God to offer your bodies as a living sacrifice holy and acceptable to God, your spiritual worship. Do not conform yourselves to this age but be transformed by the renewal of your mind, so that you may judge what is God's will, what is good, pleasing and perfect. This is the word of the Lord.

All: Thanks be to God.

A period of silent reflection or brief homily follow. On special days another reading may be added.

IV. Gospel Canticle

STAND

CANTICLE OF ZECHARIAH

ANTIPHON: Hap - py the   pure in heart,   they   shall   see   God.

Verses of the Canticle: p. 20; or the alternate setting may be used.

V. Intercessions

STAND: The ASSISTANT MINISTER/CANTOR sings the petitions, and the people sing the response after each petition.

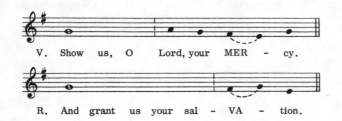

V. Show us, O   Lord, your   MER - cy.

R. And grant us your sal - VA - tion.

V: Be the protector and director/of our NAtion.

R: And in your mercy hear and an/swer our prayers.

V: Clothe your/priests in righteousness.

R: And make your chosen people/JOYful.

V: Keep your/people safe, O Lord.

R: Bless those who be/long to you.

V: Grant peace in our/TIME, O Lord.

R: Only you make us live in/SAFEty.

V: Create clean/hearts for us, O God.

R: And renew a constant spir/it in us.

Celebrant: Adorn our hearts and our hands with power and with virtue, O Lord, and surround us with the seven sanctifying gifts of your Holy Spirit that we may work and pray for your greater honor and glory; through Jesus Christ our Lord.

All: Amen.

VI. Lord's Prayer

See p. 24

VII. Blessing and Dismissal

Assistant: Let us/bless the Lord.

All: Thanks be to/God.

Celebrant: May the peace of God which passes all understanding keep our hearts and minds in Christ Je/sus our Lord.

All: A/men.

A sign of peace may be exchanged.

Thursday—Evensong

I. Light Service

STAND

ASSISTANT: Je - sus Christ is the Light of the world.

ALL: A Light no dark - ness can ex - tin - guish.

EVENING HYMN

Ach bleib bei uns
Mane nobiscum, Domine
Paraphrased, St. Joseph's
Abbey, 1967, 1968

L.M.

Old 100th
Louis Bourgeois, 1551

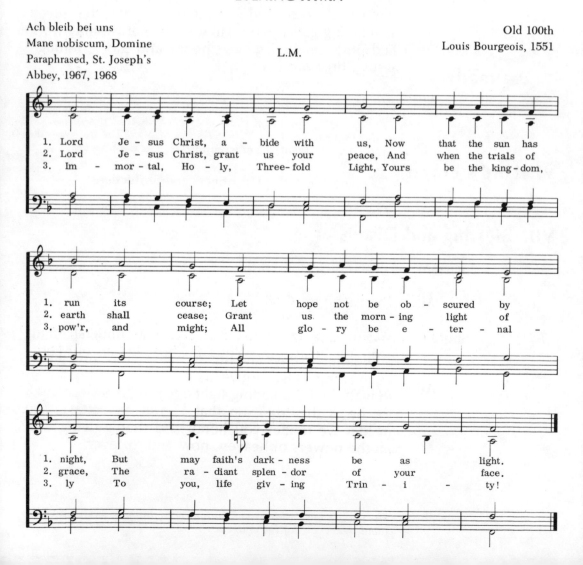

1. Lord Je - sus Christ, a - bide with us, Now that the sun has run its course; Let hope not be ob - scured by night, But may faith's dark - ness be as light.
2. Lord Je - sus Christ, grant us your peace, And when the trials of earth shall cease; Grant us the morn - ing light of grace, The ra - diant splen - dor of your face.
3. Im - mor - tal, Ho - ly, Three - fold Light, Yours be the king - dom, pow'r, and might; All glo - ry be e - ter - nal - ly To you, life giv - ing Trin - i - ty!

THANKSGIVING

Assistant: The Lord be with you.

All: And also with you.

Assistant: Blessed are you, O Lord our God, King of the universe, for your holy Name which you have planted in our hearts, and for the life, knowledge, faith and immortality which you have revealed to us through Jesus your Son. Each day of life is your gift; teach us to use it well and with grateful hearts to sing psalms, hymns and inspired canticles to the Father, the Son and the Holy Spirit, now and for ever.

All: Amen.

II. Psalmody

STAND: As Psalm 141 is sung, the CELEBRANT places incense in the thurible, and the ASSISTANT MINISTER incenses the candle, the celebrant, the other ministers, and the people.

PSALM 141—An evening prayer for forgiveness and protection

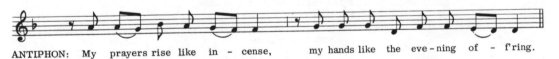

ANTIPHON: My prayers rise like in - cense, my hands like the eve-ning of - f'ring.

Psalm verses: p. 3. After the psalm is completed the celebrant begins the prayer immediately.

Celebrant: Lord God, true and eternal Light, controlling the alternation of days and nights, hear our trusting prayer as evening falls; forgive us our sins and enable us to walk in the unfading light of Jesus Christ our Lord, for he is the true Sun that knows no setting, and in him we render you honor and thanksgiving with all the powers of heaven, now and for ever.

All: Amen.

The people may sit or stand during the remaining psalmody; they stand, however, for the collects.

PSALM 121

"He who sits on the throne will give them shelter." (Revelation 7:15)

Psalm 121
The Psalter, 1912

C.M.

Dunfermline
Scottish Psalter, 1615

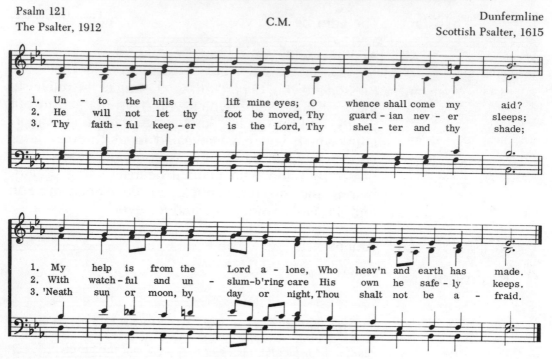

1. Un - to the hills I lift mine eyes; O whence shall come my aid?
2. He will not let thy foot be moved, Thy guard - ian nev - er sleeps;
3. Thy faith - ful keep - er is the Lord, Thy shel - ter and thy shade;

1. My help is from the Lord a - lone, Who heav'n and earth has made.
2. With watch - ful and un - slum - b'ring care His own he safe - ly keeps.
3. 'Neath sun or moon, by day or night, Thou shalt not be a - fraid.

4. From evil he will keep thee safe,
For thee he will provide;
Thy going out, thy coming in,
For ever he will guide.

Celebrant: Let us pray.

Pause for silent prayer.

Heavenly Father, you have brought us safely to the ending of this day; defend us with your mighty power that this night we may not fall into any sin nor run into any kind of danger but that under your governance we may always do what is righteous in your sight; through Jesus Christ our Lord.

All: Amen.

REVELATION 11:17–18; 12:10–12

"Christ's blood is beyond all price." (I Peter 1:18)

English version: NAB   Frank Quinn, O.P.

who   night   and   day   accused   them   be - fore   our   God.

6. They   defeated   him   by   the   blood   of   the   Lamb   and   by   the   word   of   their

tes - ti - mo - ny;   love   for   life   did   not   deter   them   from   death.

7. Glory   to   the   Father,   and   to   the   Son,   and   to   the   Ho - ly   Spir - it.

Rejoice,   you   heav - ens,   and   you   that   dwell there - in

Celebrant: Let us pray.

Pause for silent prayer.

O King of the ages, to whom men and angels sing, grant that what we sing with our lips we may believe in our hearts, and what we believe in our hearts we may practice in our lives; so that being doers of the Word and not hearers only, we may obtain everlasting life; through Jesus Christ our Lord.

All: Amen.

III. Reading

SIT

A reading from the letter of blessed Paul the Apostle to the Romans (13:8–10): Owe no debt to anyone except the debt that binds us to love one another. He who loves his neighbor has fulfilled the law. The commandments, "You shall not commit adultery; you shall not murder; you shall not steal; you shall not covet," and any other commandment there may be are all summed up in this, "You shall love your neighbor as yourself." Love never does any wrong to the neighbor, hence love is the fulfillment of the law. This is the word of the Lord.

All: Thanks be to God.

A period of silent reflection or brief homily follow. On special days another reading may be added.

IV. Gospel Canticle

STAND

CANTICLE OF MARY

ANTIPHON: Re - joice, so high - ly fa - vored, the Lord is with you.

Verses of the Canticle: p. 8. The alternate setting of the Canticle may be used, or one of the settings of the Canticle of Simeon.

V. Intercessions

STAND: The ASSISTANT MINISTER/CANTOR sings the petitions, and the people sing the response after each petition.

1. In peace, let us pray to the Lord.

R: Lord, have mercy.

2. For the Church universal, its ministries and its continuing renewal, let us pray to the Lord.

3. For our country, for all nations and for peace in the world, let us pray to the Lord.

4. For the continuing work of creation and for man's creative vision and inventive skill, let us pray to the Lord.

5. For the tempted and despairing, the sick and the handicapped and the ministries of care and healing, let us pray to the Lord.

6. For all that sets men free from pain, fear and distress, let us pray to the Lord.

7. For the assurance God's mercy knows no limit, let us pray to the Lord.

8. For those who mourn that all tears be wiped away by the mystery of the Cross, let us pray to the Lord.

9. For refreshment, light and peace for the faithful departed, let us pray to the Lord.

10. Help, save, pity and defend us, O God, by your grace. *(Pause)*

11. Rejoicing in the fellowship of the Blessed Virgin Mary, of St. *Name,* and of all the saints, let us commend ourselves, one another and our whole life to Christ our Lord.

R: To you, O Lord.

Celebrant: Almighty God, our heavenly Father, who purchased for yourself a universal Church by the precious blood of your dear Son; mercifully look upon the same and so guide and govern the minds and hearts of both pastors and people that we may set forth your glory by word and deed and forward the salvation of all men; through the same Jesus Christ our Lord.

All: Amen.

VI. Lord's Prayer

See p. 34

VII. Blessing and Dismissal

The ASSISTANT MINISTER sings:

Assistant: Bow down your heads to the Lord.

With raised hand the CELEBRANT imparts a blessing.

Celebrant: May God the King of the universe bless you and keep / you.

All: Amen.

Celebrant: May the master of life and of death graciously smi-le / upon you.

All: Amen.

Celebrant: May the / Lord grant you peace.

All: Amen.

A sign of peace may be exchanged.

Friday—Morning Prayer

I. Invitatory

STAND

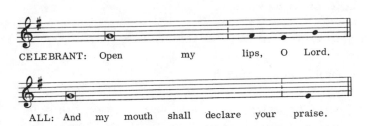

CELEBRANT: Open my lips, O Lord.

ALL: And my mouth shall declare your praise.

MORNING HYMN

P. Brennan, C.SS.R., alt.
Westminster Hymnal

77.77.D

St. George's Windsor
G. J. Elvey, 1816–93

1. Hail, Re-deem - er, King di - vine! Priest and Lamb, the throne is thine;
2. Christ, thou King of truth and might, Be to us e - ter - nal light,

1. King whose reign shall nev - er cease, Prince of ev - er - last - ing peace.
2. Till in peace each na - tion rings With thy prais - es, King of kings.

An - gels, saints, and na - tions sing: "Praised be Je - sus Christ, our King;

Lord of earth and sky and sea, King of love on Cal - va - ry.

Celebrant: The Lord be with you.

All: And also with you.

The prayer follows immediately.

Celebrant: Lord Jesus Christ, sun of righteousness, open our eyes and turn us from darkness to light and from the dominion of Satan to God, that we may receive the forgiveness of our sins and a place among those made holy by faith in your cross, O Savior of the world, who live and reign for ever and ever.

All: Amen.

II. Psalmody

The people may sit during the first two psalms; they stand, however, for the collects and the Psalm of Praise.

PSALM 51—Contrition for sin

English version: Grail   Frank Quinn, O.P.

ANTIPHON: A hum - bled, con - trite heart you will not spurn.

1. HAVE MER - / cy on me / God, in your kind - ness. *
   O wash me more and more from my guilt *

In your compassion blot / out my of - FENSE.
and cleanse / me from my SIN.

2. My offences / truly I know them; * my sin is / always before me.
    Against you, you alone / HAVE I sinned; * what is evil in your / sight I have DONE.

3. That you may be justified when / you give sentence * and be without re / proach when you JUDGE,
    O see, in guilt / I was born, * a sinner was / I conCEIVED.

4. Indeed you love / truth in the heart; * then in the secret of my heart / TEACH me wisdom.
    O purify me, then / I shall be clean; * O wash me, I shall be / whiter than SNOW.

5. Make me hear re / joicing and gladness, * that the bones you have / CRUSHED may THRILL.
    From my sins turn / aWAY your face * and blot / out all my GUILT.

6. A pure heart create for / ME, O God, * put a steadfast / spirit within me.
    Do not cast me a / way from your presence, * nor deprive me of your / HOly spirit.

7. Give me again the / joy of your help; * with a spirit of / fervor sustain me,
    that I may teach trans / gressors your ways * and sinners may re / TURN to YOU.

8. Glory to the Father, and to the Son, and to the / HOly Spirit: *
    As in the beginning, so now and for / ever. A - MEN.

Celebrant: Let us pray.

Pause for silent prayer.

Almighty and merciful Father, you freely forgive those who acknowledge and confess their sins, as did David the prophet; create pure hearts in us, O God, and wash away all our sins in the precious blood of your dear Son, our Savior Jesus Christ, who lives and reigns with you and the Holy Spirit, one God, for ever and ever.

All: Amen.

JONAH 2:2–9
"The sign of the prophet Jonah" (Mt 12:39)

English version: NAB   Frank Quinn, O.P.

ANTIPHON: Fa - ther,   in - to your hands,   I   com-mend my   spir - it.

1. Out of my distress I called to the Lord, and he answered me; From the

midst of the nether world I cried for help, and you heard my voice

2. For you cast me into the deep, into the heart of the sea, and the flood en-veloped me;

All your breakers and your billows passed o - ver me.

3. Then I said, "I am banished from your sight! yet would I again look up-

on your holy tem - ple." The waters swirled about me, threatening my life;

the abyss en - veloped me; seaweed clung a - bout my head.

4. Down I went to the roots of the mountains; the bars of the nether world were closing behind

me for - ev - er. But you brought up my life from the pit, O Lord, my God.

5. When my soul fainted with-in me, I re-membered the Lord;

My prayer reached you in your holy tem - ple.

6. Those who worship vain idols for-sake their source of mer - cy.

But I, with resounding praise, will sacrifice to you;

What I have vowed I will pay; deliverance is from the Lord.

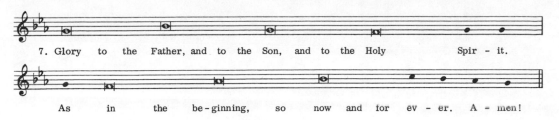

7. Glory to the Father, and to the Son, and to the Holy Spir - it.

As in the be - ginning, so now and for ev - er. A - men!

Celebrant: Let us pray.

Pause for silent prayer.

O God of heaven, who made the sea and the land, as the prophet Jonah was a sign to the Ninevites, so make the Son of Man, our Lord Jesus Christ, a sign to this generation; by his descent among the dead and by his glorious resurrection on the third day, rescue us from the abyss of sin, renew this world of yours and flood our minds with light; through the same Christ our Lord.

All: Amen.

STAND

PSALM 149—Praise God in all his saints

Psalm 149
The Psalter, 1912

C.M.

St. Flavian
Day's Psalter, 1563

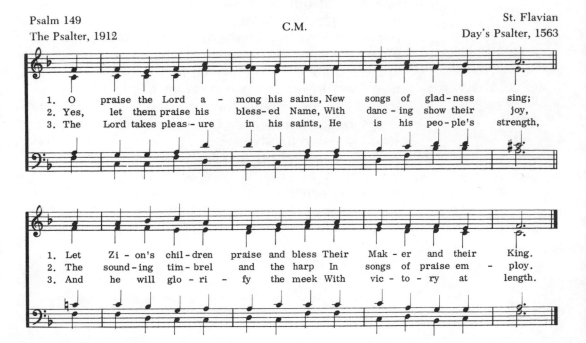

1. O praise the Lord a - mong his saints, New songs of glad-ness sing;
2. Yes, let them praise his bless-ed Name, With danc - ing show their joy,
3. The Lord takes pleas - ure in his saints, He is his peo-ple's strength,

1. Let Zi - on's chil - dren praise and bless Their Mak - er and their King.
2. The sound - ing tim - brel and the harp In songs of praise em - ploy.
3. And he will glo - ri - fy the meek With vic - to - ry at length.

4. You saints, by day and night rejoice,
    Exult and joyful stand,
    The Lord's great praises in your mouth,
    His sword within your hand.

5. This is the glorious judgment giv'n:
    His saints shall rule the earth;
    Then bless the Lord, his glory tell,
    And celebrate his worth.

Celebrant: Let us pray.

Pause for silent prayer.

Merciful God, Friend of mankind, it is our duty and our delight to worship you in the beauty of holiness and serve you as Lord and Creator; praise and glory are your due from all, Father, Son and Holy Spirit, now and for ever.

All: Amen.

III. Reading

SIT

A reading from the letter to the Hebrews (4:14–5:7–9): Since we have a great high priest who has passed through the heavens, Jesus, the Son of God, let us hold fast to our profession of faith. For we do not have a high priest who is unable to sympathize with our weakness, but one who was tempted in every way that we are, yet never sinned. So let us confidently approach the throne of grace to receive mercy and favor and to find help in time of need. . . . In the days when he was in the flesh, he offered prayers and supplications with loud cries and tears to God, who was able to save him from death, and he was heard because of his reverence. Son though he was, he learned obedience from what he suffered; and when perfected, he became the source of eternal salvation for all who obey him. This is the word of the Lord.

All: Thanks be to God.

A period of silent reflection or brief homily follow. On special days another reading may be added.

IV. Gospel Canticle

STAND

CANTICLE OF ZECHARIAH

Verses of the Canticle: p. 20; or the alternate setting may be used.

V. Intercessions

STAND: The ASSISTANT MINISTER/CANTOR sings the petitions, and the people sing the response after each petition.

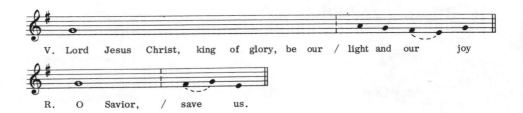

V: By the divine power of the precious and/LIFE-giving Cross.

R: O Savior,/SAVE us.

V: By your glorious resurrection and/wonderful ascension.

R: O Savior,/SAVE us.

V: By the coming of the/ParaCLETE Spirit.

R: O Savior,/SAVE us.

V: By the sacred mysteries of our baptism/and the holy eucharist.

R: O Savior,/SAVE us.

Other petitions may be added.

Celebrant: Lord Jesus Christ, who loved us and offered yourself up for us as an agreeable and fragrant sacrifice to God, deliver us from our former darkness and teach us to conduct ourselves as children of the light in all goodness, justice and truth; you live and reign for ever and ever.

All: Amen.

VI. Lord's Prayer

See p. 24

VII. Blessing and Dismissal

Assistant: Let us/bless the Lord.

All: Thanks be to/God.

Celebrant: May Christ our true God, by the power of his holy cross, have mercy on/us and save us.

All: A/men.

A sign of peace may be exchanged.

Friday—Evensong

I. Light Service

STAND

ASSISTANT: Je - sus Christ is the light of the world.

ALL: A light no dark - ness can ex - tin - guish.

EVENING HYMN

Thomas Ken, 1709, alt.

L.M.

Illsley
J. Bishop, c. 1665–1737

1. All praise to you, O God, this night, For
2. For - give us, Lord, through Christ your Son, What -
3. En - light - en us, O bless - ed Light, And

1. all the bless - ings of the light, Keep us, we pray, O
2. ev - er wrong this day we've done; Your peace give to the
3. give us rest through - out this night. O strength - en us, that

1. King of kings, Be - neath your own al - might - y wings
2. world, O Lord, That man might live in one ac - cord.
3. for your sake, We all may serve you when we wake,

4. All glory be to you, O Lord,
   The Virgin's Son, by all adored:
   And equal praise forever greet
   The Father and the Paraclete.

THANKSGIVING

Assistant: The Lord be with you.

All: And also with you.

Assistant: Blessed are you, O Lord, our God, King of the universe, the giver of every good and perfect gift; fill us with your Spirit and enable us to sing psalms, hymns and inspired canticles when we come together, and to go on singing and chanting to the Lord in our hearts, so that always and everywhere and for every gift we may give thanks to God our Father in the name of our Lord Jesus Christ; who lives and reigns for ever and ever.

All: Amen.

II. Psalmody

STAND: As Psalm 141 is sung, the CELEBRANT places incense in the thurible, and the ASSISTANT MINISTER incenses the candle, the celebrant, the other ministers, and the people.

PSALM 141—An evening prayer for forgiveness and protection

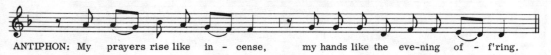

ANTIPHON: My   prayers rise like   in - cense,   my hands like the   eve-ning   of - f'ring.

Psalm verses: p. 3. After the psalm is completed the celebrant begins the prayer immediately.

Celebrant: Almighty and everlasting God, may our prayers rise like incense before you, our hands like an evening sacrifice; as we contemplate your presence in Word and Sacrament and in the lives of our brothers, rekindle in us the fire of that love which Jesus your Son lit on earth by his passion and which burns in our hearts by the Holy Spirit; you are one God through all the ages of ages.

All: Amen.

The people may sit or stand during the remaining psalmody; they stand, however, for the collects.

PSALM 130
"He will save his people from their sins." (Mt 1:21)

English version: J. F. Cunningham, O.P.

Adap. Rev. M. Quinn, O.P. et al

87.87.887

Aus Tiefer Not

Walther's *Geistliche Gesangbuchlein*, Wittenberg, 1524

1. Out of the depths I cry, O Lord, To you I cry for mer - cy. Hear me, O Lord, hear now my voice And grant my prayer for mer - cy. For if you num - ber sins, and shame, If you re - cord each sin - ner's name, What man dare stand be - fore you?

2. But with you is for - give - ness, Lord, Your law, which gives sal - va - tion. And in that word my soul stands firm And hopes for its sal - va - tion. Though days be long from dawn's first light Un - to the watch which guards the night, The Lord shall be our help - er.

3. His lov - ing kind - ness gives us hope Of plen - te - ous re - dem - tion. The Lord shall free his Is - ra - el, From sin he brings re - demp - tion. Now glo - ry be to God the Lord, Most ho - ly Trin - i - ty a - dored Of Fa - ther, Son, and Spir - it.

Celebrant: Let us pray.

Pause for silent prayer.

Guard us while we are awake, O Lord, and keep us while we sleep, that waking we may watch with Christ and sleeping we may rest in peace; through the same Jesus Christ our Lord.

All: Amen.

REVELATION 15:3–4—A hymn of adoration

English version: NAB   Frank Quinn, O.P.

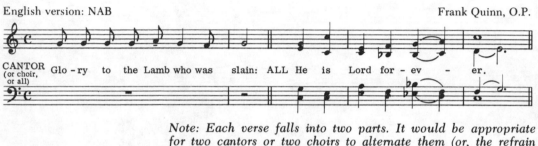

CANTOR (or choir, or all)   Glo-ry to the Lamb who was slain: ALL He is Lord for-ev-er.

Note: Each verse falls into two parts. It would be appropriate for two cantors or two choirs to alternate them (or, the refrain may be added after each half-verse).

1a. Might-y and won-der-ful are your works, · Lord God Al-might-y!

1b. Right-eous and true are your ways, O King of the na-tions.

2a. Who would dare re-fuse you hon-or, or the glo-ry due your name, O Lord?

2b. Since you a-lone are ho-ly, all na-tions shall come and wor-ship in

your pres-ence. Your might-y deeds are clear-ly seen.

3a. Glo-ry to the Fa-ther, and to the Son, and to the Ho-ly Spir-it.

3b. As in the be-gin-ning, so now and for ev-er. A-men.

Celebrant: Let us pray.

Pause for silent prayer.

Grant, O Father, that as we are baptized 'into the death of your beloved Son, our Savior Jesus Christ, so by continually dying to our corrupt affections, we may be buried with him, and through the grave and gate of death may pass to our joyful resurrection; for his merits, who died and was buried and rose again for us, the same Jesus Christ our Lord.

All: Amen.

III. Reading

SIT

A reading from the first letter of blessed John the Apostle (4:7–11): Beloved, let us love one another because love is of God; everyone who loves is begotten of God and has knowledge of God. The man without love has known nothing of God, for God is love. God's love was revealed in our midst in this way: he sent his only Son to the world that we might have life through him. Love, then, consists in this: not that we have loved God, but that he has loved us and has sent his Son as an offering for our sins. Beloved, if God has loved us so, we must have the same love for one another. This is the word of the Lord.

All: Thanks be to God.

A period of silent reflection or brief homily follow. On special days another reading may be added.

IV. Gospel Canticle

STAND

CANTICLE OF MARY

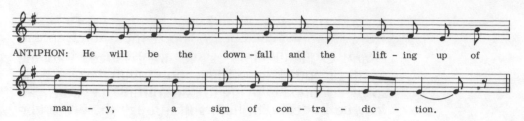

ANTIPHON: He will be the down-fall and the lift-ing up of man-y, a sign of con-tra-dic-tion.

Verses of the Canticle: p. 8. The alternate setting of the Canticle may be used, or one of the settings of the Canticle of Simeon.

V. Intercessions

STAND: The ASSISTANT MINISTER/CANTOR sings the petitions, and the people sing the response after each petition.

1. In peace, let us pray to the Lord.

R: Lord, have mercy.

2. For zeal in the Lord's service that all our thoughts and actions may be for his glory, let us pray to the Lord.
3. For heart-felt sympathy for the needs of our brothers that fraternal affection never fail them, let us pray to the Lord.
4. For good and honest hearts and a clean conscience before God, let us pray to the Lord.
5. For the building of a more human world and a respect for all human needs, let us pray to the Lord.
6. For the comforting of those who suffer in mind and body and for peace for the dying, let us pray to the Lord.
7. For all those who have gone before us through the gates of death and whose names are written in the book of life, let us pray to the Lord.
8. Help, save, pity and defend us, O God, by your grace. *(Pause)*
9. Rejoicing in the fellowship of the Blessed Virgin Mary, of St. *Name,* and of all the saints, let us commend ourselves, one another and our whole life to Christ our Lord.

R: To you, O Lord.

Celebrant: Lord God, stretch out the right hand of your majesty over your holy, catholic and apostolic Church spread abroad throughout the world; preserve it from all harm, visible and invisible, and through your mercy make us worthy to serve you in purity of heart and devotion of life; through Jesus Christ our Lord.

All: Amen.

VI. Lord's Prayer

See p. 34

VII. Blessing and Dismissal

The ASSISTANT MINISTER sings:

Assistant: Bow down your heads to the Lord.

With raised hand the CELEBRANT imparts a blessing.

Celebrant: May God the King of the universe bless you and keep / you.

All: Amen.

Celebrant: May the master of life and of death graciously smile / upon you.

All: Amen.

Celebrant: May the / Lord grant you peace.

All: Amen.

A sign of peace may be exchanged.

Saturday—Morning Prayer

I. Invitatory

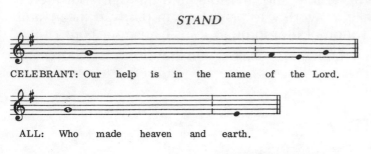

STAND

CELEBRANT: Our help is in the name of the Lord.

ALL: Who made heaven and earth.

MORNING HYMN

John S. Monsell, 1863, alt.   Han van Koert

L.M.

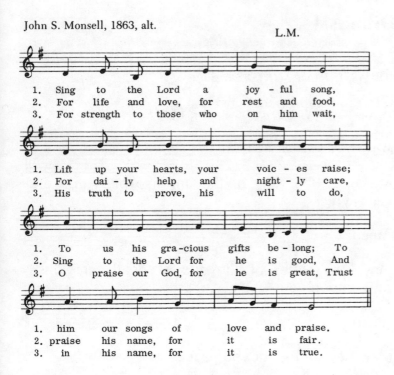

1. Sing to the Lord a joy-ful song,
2. For life and love, for rest and food,
3. For strength to those who on him wait,

1. Lift up your hearts, your voic-es raise;
2. For dai-ly help and night-ly care,
3. His truth to prove, his will to do,

1. To us his gra-cious gifts be-long; To
2. Sing to the Lord for he is good, And
3. O praise our God, for he is great, Trust

1. him our songs of love and praise.
2. praise his name, for it is fair.
3. in his name, for it is true.

4. For joys untold, that from above
   Cheer those who love his sweet employ,
   Sing to our God, for he is love,
   Exalt his name, for it is joy.

5. For he is Lord of heav'n and earth,
   Whom angels serve and saints adore;
   And he has blessed us from our birth:
   To him be praise for evermore.

Celebrant: The Lord be with you.

All: And also with you.

The prayer follows immediately.

Celebrant: O God, who first ordered light to shine in darkness, flood our hearts with the glorious Gospel of Christ, your matchless image, and transform us more and more into his very likeness; through the same Jesus Christ our Lord.

All: Amen.

II. Psalmody

The people may sit during the first two psalms; they stand, however, for the collects and the Psalm of Praise.

PSALM 30—Sorrow transmuted into joy

English version: Grail   Frank Quinn, O.P.

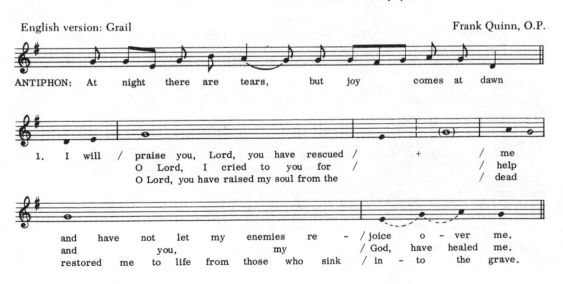

ANTIPHON: At night there are tears, but joy comes at dawn

1.   I will / praise you, Lord, you have rescued /   + / me
     O Lord, I cried to you for /   / help
     O Lord, you have raised my soul from the /   / dead

     and have not let my enemies re - / joice o - ver me.
     and   you,   my   / God, have healed me.
     restored me to life from those who sink / in - to the grave.

2.   Sing psalms to the Lord, you who / love him, * give thanks to his / HOly name.
     His anger lasts but a mo / ment; + his favor all through / life. *
     At night there are tears, but / joy comes with dawn.

3.   I said to myself in my good / fortune: * "Nothing will ev / er disturb me."
     Your favor had set me on a mountain / fastness, *
     then you hid your face and I was put / to confusion.

4. To you, Lord, I / cried * to my God I / MADE appeal:
   "What profit would my death be, my going to the / grave? *
   Can dust give you praise or pro / CLAIM your truth?"

5. The Lord listened and had / pity. * The Lord / came to my help.
   For me you have changed my mourning into / dancing, *
   you removed my sackcloth and gir / dled me with joy.

6. So my soul sings psalms to you un / ceasingly. * O Lord my God, I will thank you / for EVer.
   Glory to the Father, and to the Son, and to the Holy / Spirit: *
   As in the beginning, so now and for ev / er. A - men.

Celebrant: Let us pray.

Pause for silent prayer.

Lord Jesus Christ, your cross is the tree of life planted in the midst of your holy church; by its saving power change our mourning into joy and enable us to sing psalms to you unceasingly, O Savior of the world, who live and reign with the Father and the Holy Spirit, one God, for ever and ever.

All: Amen.

EXODUS 15:1–4, 8–13, 17–18—The victory song of Moses and of Miriam

English version: NAB   Frank Quinn, O.P.

ANTIPHON: Great and won-der-ful are your deeds, Lord God al - might - y.

1. I will sing to the Lord, for he is glo-ri-ous-ly tri-um-phant; horse and char-i-ot he has cast in-to the sea.

2. My strength and my cour-age is the Lord, and he has been my sav - ior. He is my God, I praise him; the God of my fa-ther, I ex-tol him.

3. The Lord is a war-rior, Lord is his name!

Pha-raoh's char-i-ots and ar-my he hurled in-to the sea.

4. At a breath of your an-ger the wa-ters pilled

up, the flow-ing wa-ters stood like a mound, the

flood wa-ters con-gealed in the midst of the sea.

5. The en-e-my boast-ed, "I will pur-sue and o-ver-

take them; I will di-vide the spoils and have my fill of them;

I will draw my sword; my hand shall de-spoil them."

6. When your wind blew, the sea cov-ered them; like lead they, sank in the might-y

wa-ters. Who is like to you a-mong the gods, O

Lord? Who is like to you, mag-nif-i-cent in ho-li-ness?

7. O ter-ri-ble in re-nown, work-er of won-ders,

when you stretched out your right hand, the earth swal-lowed them!

In your mer-cy you led the peo-ple you re-deemed; in your

strength you guid-ed them to your ho-ly dwell - ing.

8. And you brought them in and plant-ed them on the moun-tain of your in-her-i-tance the place where you made your seat, O Lord.

The sanc-tu-ar-y, O Lord, which your hands es-tab-lished. The Lord shall reign for ev-er and ev-er.

Glo-ry to the Fa - ther, and to the Son, and to the Ho-ly Spir - it. As in the be-gin-ning, so now and for ev - er. A - men.

Celebrant: Let us pray.

Pause for silent prayer.

O King of the nations and Redeemer of your people, we reverence and praise your name, for you alone are holy; continue to perform your acts of justice on behalf of the poor and afflicted and rescue your Church from the malice of its enemies; through Christ our Lord.

All: Amen.

STAND

PSALM 150—The Grand Doxology

James Quinn, S.J., 1969

S.M.D.

Diademata

G. J. Elvey, 1816–93

1. Bless'd be the Lord our God! With joy let heav-en ring; Be-
2. All that has life and breath, Give thanks with heart-felt songs! To

1. fore his pres-ence let all earth Its songs of hom-age bring! His
2. him let all cre-a-tion sing To whom all praise be-longs! Ac-

1. might-y deeds be told; His maj-es-ty be praised; To
2. claim the Fa-ther's love, Who gave us God his Son; Praise

1. God, en-throned in heav'n-ly light, Let ev'-ry voice be raised!
2. too the Spir-it, giv'n by both, With both for ev-er one!

Celebrant: Let us pray.

Pause for silent prayer.

Heavenly Father, in our sacrifice of praise we cherish the sacred memory of the Virgin-Mother of your Son, our Savior Jesus Christ, and of all your saints of every time and place; as we unite our prayers with theirs, join us with the whole blessed company of heaven that with them we may offer you worthy praise and thanksgiving, now and always and for ever and ever.

All: Amen.

III. Reading

SIT

A reading from the letter of blessed Paul the Apostle to the Philippians (3:8–14): I have come to rate all as loss in the light of the surpassing knowledge of my Lord Jesus Christ. For his sake I have forfeited everything; I have accounted all else rubbish so that Christ may be my wealth and I may be in him, not having any justice of my own based on observance of the law. The justice I possess is that which comes through faith in Christ. It has its origin in God and is based on faith. I wish to know Christ and the power flowing from his resurrection; likewise to know how to share in his sufferings by being formed into the pattern of his death. Thus do I hope that I may arrive at resurrection from the dead. This is the word of the Lord.

All: Thanks be to God.

A period of silent reflection or brief homily follow. On special days another reading may be added.

IV. Gospel Canticle

STAND

CANTICLE OF ZECHARIAH

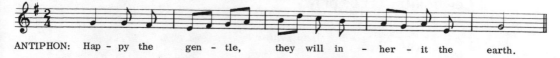

ANTIPHON: Hap - py the   gen - tle,   they will in - her - it the   earth.

Verses of the Canticle: p. 20; or the alternate setting may be used.

V. Intercessions

STAND: The ASSISTANT MINISTER/CANTOR sings the petitions, and the people sing the response after each petition.

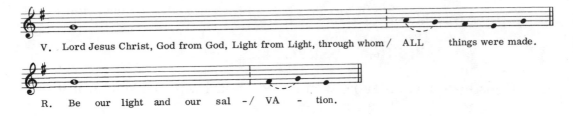

V. Lord Jesus Christ, God from God, Light from Light, through whom / ALL   things were made.

R.   Be   our   light   and   our   sal -/ VA - tion.

V: Lord Jesus Christ, Source of / life and holiness.

R: Be our light and our sal / VAtion.

V: Lord Jesus Christ, make your Church faithful to the / LIGHT of the Gospel.

R: Be our light and our sal / VAtion.

V: Lord Jesus Christ, prosper the work of our / HANDS FOR us.

R: Be our light and our sal / VAtion.

V: Lord Jesus Christ, make us the salt of the earth and the / LIGHT of the world.

R: Be our light and our sal / VAtion.

Other petitions may be added

Celebrant: Lord Jesus Christ, who willingly accepted crucifixion for the resurrection of mankind, save your people and bless your inheritance, grant faith to the living and rest to the departed, and bring us safely to our heavenly home, where we shall praise you in union with all your saints, for ever and ever.

All: Amen.

VI. Lord's Prayer

See p. 24

VII. Blessing and Dismissal

Assistant: Let us/bless the Lord.

All: Thanks be to/God.

Celebrant: May he who is good and loves mankind, Christ our true God, bless/us and keep us.

All: A/men.

A sign of peace may be exchanged.

Proper of the Seasons

Advent
Christmas
Lent
Easter

Holy Mother Church is conscious that she must celebrate the saving work of her divine Spouse by devoutly recalling it on certain days throughout the course of the year. Every week, on the day which she has called the Lord's day, she keeps the memory of the Lord's resurrection, which she also celebrates once in the year, together with his blessed passion, in the most solemn festival of Easter.
Within the cycle of a year, moreover, she unfolds the whole mystery of Christ, from the incarnation and birth until the ascension, the day of Pentecost, and the expectation of blessed hope and of the coming of the Lord. Recalling thus the mysteries of redemption, the Church opens to the faithful the riches of her Lord's powers and merits, so that these are in some way made present for all time, and the faithful are enabled to lay hold upon them and become filled with saving grace.
The Constitution on the Sacred Liturgy, 102

Advent—Evensong

EVENING HYMN

Creator Alme Siderum, 7th
Tr. Melvin Farrell, S.S.

L.M.

Plainsong

1. O Lord of light, who made the stars, O Dawn by whom we see the Way,
2. In low-li-ness you came on earth To res-cue man from Sa-tan's snares:
3. To pay the dept we owed for sin Your pain-ful cross was named the price;

1. O Christ Re-deem-er of all men, Make haste to lis-ten as we pray!
2. O won-drous Love that healed our wounds By tak-ing on our mor-tal cares!
3. From Mar-y's vir-gin-shrine you came A spot-less host for sac-ri-fice.

4. But now you reign the King of kings,
   Adored in highest majesty;
   Your very name commands respect
   From pole to pole and sea to sea!

5. Great judge of mankind's final day
   Have pity on your children's plight:
   Rise up to shield us with your grace,
   Deliver us from Satan's might,

6. To God the Father and the Son
   For ages of eternal days
   Together with the Spirit be
   All glory, honor, might, and praise!

Readings

To Dec. 16: A Reading From The Prophet Isaiah (42:1–7): Here is my servant whom I uphold, my chosen one with whom I am pleased, upon whom I have put my spirit: he shall bring forth justice to the nations, not crying out, not shouting, not making his voice heard in the street. A bruised reed he shall not break, and a smoldering wick he shall not quench, until he establishes justice on the earth. . . . I, the Lord, have called you from the victory of justice, I have grasped you by the hand; I formed you, and set you as a covenant of the people, a light for the nations, to open the eyes of the blind, to bring out prisoners from confinement, and from the dungeon, those who live in darkness. This is the word of the Lord.

All: Thanks be to God.

Dec. 17–23: A Reading From The Prophet Isaiah (11:1–6): A shoot shall sprout from the stump of Jesse, and from his roots a bud shall blossom. The Spirit of the Lord shall rest upon him: a spirit of wisdom and of understanding, a spirit of counsel and of strength, a spirit of knowledge and of fear of the Lord, and his delight shall be the fear of the Lord. Not by appearance shall he judge, nor by hearsay shall he decide, but he shall judge the poor with justice, and decide aright for the land's afflicted. He shall strike the ruthless with the rod of his mouth, and with the breath of his lips he shall slay the wicked. Justice shall be the band around his waist, and faithfulness a belt upon his hips. Then the wolf shall be a guest of the lamb, and the leopard shall lie down with the kid; the calf and the young lion shall browse together, with a little child to guide them. This is the word of the Lord.

All: Thanks be to God.

Gospel Canticle

CANTICLE OF MARY

Week 1

1. The Holy Spir - it shall come up - on you and the power of the Most High' shall o - ver shad - ow you.

Week 2

2. Come, Lord, vis - it us with your peace.

Week 3

3. Show us, O Lord, your mer - cy, and grant us your sal - va - tion.

Week 4

4. He shall reign for ev – er and ev – er.

Intercessions

CANTOR: Come and save us, ALL: Come and save us. HARMONY: Come and save us.

1. O Wisdom, breath of the Most High, pervading and perme – at – ing all cre – a – tion,

2. O Lord of lords and Leader of the house of Is – ra – el,

who appeared to Moses in the burning bush and gave him the Law on Si – nai,

3. O Root of Jesse, standing as a signal to the na – tions, be – fore whom all

kings are mute, to whom the na – tions will do hom – age,

4. O Key of David and Ruler of the house of Is – ra – el, who

opens and no man can close, who closes and no man can o – pen,

5. O radiant Dawn, Splendor of e – ter – nal light and

Sun of justice to those who live in dark – ness and in the shad – ow of death,

6. O King of the na - tions, the Ruler they long for, the Cornerstone bringing all men to - geth - er,

7. O Emmanuel, our King and our Law giv - er, the A - nointed of the na - tions and their Sav - ior,

Collect: O God our Father, each year you fill us with joy as we recall the mysteries of our redemption and look forward to the great day of our final salvation. Grant that as we joyfully remember your Son's first appearing among us as our Savior, we may one day see him without dread when he returns as our Judge; through the same Jesus Christ our Lord.

All: Amen.

Blessing

1. May Jesus Christ, Son of God and Son of Mary, bless you and keep/you.

R: Amen.

2. May the Lord who comes to judge the living and the dead graciously smile/upon you.

R: Amen.

3. May the/Lord grant you peace.

R: Amen.

Advent—Morning Prayer

Invitatory

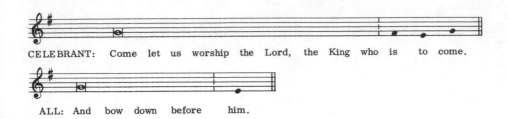

CELEBRANT: Come let us worship the Lord, the King who is to come.

ALL: And bow down before him.

MORNING HYMN

Greek: Tr. John Brownlie, 1907
"Hymns of the Russian Church"—
Oxford University Press

C.M.

St. Peter
A. R. Reinagle, 1799-1877

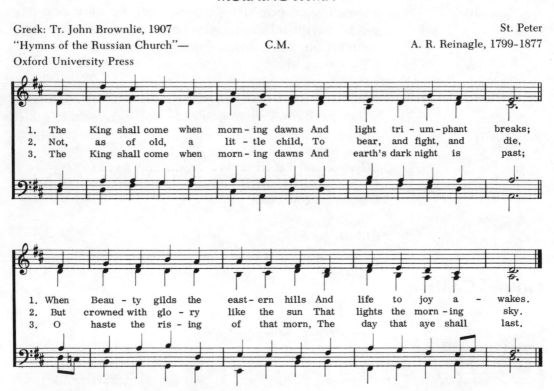

1. The King shall come when morn-ing dawns And light tri-um-phant breaks;
2. Not, as of old, a lit-tle child, To bear, and fight, and die,
3. The King shall come when morn-ing dawns And earth's dark night is past;

1. When Beau-ty gilds the east-ern hills And life to joy a-wakes.
2. But crowned with glo-ry like the sun That lights the morn-ing sky.
3. O haste the ris-ing of that morn, The day that aye shall last.

4. And let the endless bliss begin,
   By weary saints foretold,
   When right shall triumph over wrong,
   And truth shall be extolled.

5. The King shall come when morning dawns
   And light and beauty brings:
   Hail, Christ the Lord! Thy people pray,
   Come quickly, King of kings.

Readings

To Dec. 16:   A Reading From the Letter Of Blessed Paul The Apostle To The Romans (13:11–14): It is now the hour for you to wake from sleep, for our salvation is closer than when we first accepted the faith. The night is far spent; the day draws near. Let us cast off deeds of darkness and put on the armor of light. Let us live honorably as in the daylight; not in carousing and drunkenness, not in sexual excess and lust, not in quarreling and jealousy. Rather, put on the Lord Jesus Christ and make no provision for the desires of the flesh. This is the word of the Lord.

All: Thanks be to God.

Dec. 17–24:   A Reading From The Prophet Isaiah (9:1–6): The people who walked in darkness have seen a great light; upon those who dwelt in the land of gloom a light has shone. . . . For a child is born to us, a son is given us; upon his shoulder dominion rests. They name him Wonder-Counselor, God-Hero, Father-Forever, Prince of Peace. His dominion is vast and forever peaceful, from David's throne, and over his kingdom, which he confirms and sustains by judgment and justice, both now and forever. The zeal of the Lord of hosts will do this! This is the word of the Lord.

All: Thanks be to God.

Gospel Canticle

CANTICLE OF ZECHARIAH

Week 1

The Lord comes from a-far; all the earth is full of his glo - ry.

Week 2

The Sav - ior comes and with him all his saints.

Week 3

The dawn from on high shall break up - on us.

Week 4

Come, Lord, show us your face and we shall be saved.

Intercessions

1. Lord Jesus Christ, Son of/God and Son of Mary.

R: Come, Lord/JEsus.

2. Shine on those who dwell in darkness and the/SHAdow of death.

3. Guide our feet/on the road to peace.

4. Come and/make all THINGS new.

5. Come in our/LIVES and our labors.

6. Establish us in/righteousness and peace.

7. Save us on the/great and final day.

Collect: Pour forth, O Lord, your grace into our hearts, that we to whom the incarnation of Christ your Son was made known by the message of an angel, may by his passion and cross be brought to the glory of his resurrection; through the same Christ our Lord.

All: Amen.

Blessing

May our great God and Savior who will come again in glory on the clouds of heaven, bless/us and keep us.

All: A/men.

Christmas—Evensong

EVENING HYMN

Based on Isaiah 9
J. Morrison, 1770, alt.

C.M.

Dundee
Scottish Psalter, 1615

1. The peo-ple who in dark-ness dwelt A glo-rious light have seen;
2. To hail thee, Sun of Right-eous-ness, The gath-'ring na-tions come;
3. For un-to us a Child is born, To us a Son is giv'n;

1. The light has shone on them who long In shades of death have been.
2. They joy as when the reap-ers bear Their har-vest treas-ures home.
3. And on his shoul-der ev-er rests All pow'r in earth and heav'n.

4. His name shall be the Prince of Peace,
   The everlasting Lord,
   The Wonderful, the Counselor,
   The God by all adored.

5. His righteous government and pow'r
   Shall over all extend;
   On judgment and justice based,
   His reign shall have no end.

6. Lord Jesus, reign in us, we pray,
   And make us thine alone,
   Who with the Father ever art,
   And Holy Spirit, One.

Reading

A Reading From The First Letter of Blessed John The Evangelist (1:1–3): This is what we proclaim to you: what was from the beginning, what we have heard, what we have seen with our eyes, what we have looked upon and our hands have touched—we speak of the word of life. This life became visible; we have seen and bear witness to it, and we proclaim to you the eternal life that was present to the Father and became visible to us. What we have seen and heard we proclaim in turn to you so that you may share life with us. This fellowship of ours is with the Father and with his Son, Jesus Christ. This is the word of the Lord.

All: Thanks be to God.

Gospel Canticle

CANTICLE OF MARY

The Lord has made known his sal - va - tion, al - le - lu - ia.

Intercessions

1. In peace, let us pray to the Lord.

R: Lord, have mercy.

2. By the wedding of the human and divine natures in Christ Jesus, let us pray to the Lord.

3. By the holy mysteries of the Word made flesh, let us pray to the Lord.

4. By the wondrous birth of the timeless Son of God from the womb of the Virgin-Mother Mary, let us pray to the Lord.

5. By the humble nativity of the King of glory in the cave of Bethlehem, let us pray to the Lord.

6. By the splendid manifestation of the King of the Jews to the shepherds and the magi, let us pray to the Lord.

7. By the lowly submission of the Maker of the world to Mary and Joseph of Nazareth, let us pray to the Lord.

8. By the blessed baptism of the spotless Son of God by John in the Jordan, let us pray to the Lord.

9. By the revealing miracle of the water made wine at Cana of Galilee, let us pray to the Lord.

10. For all orthodox believers who put their trust in the incarnate Son of God, let us pray to the Lord.

11. For the conversion of the whole human race to our blessed Lord and Savior Jesus Christ, let us pray to the Lord.

12. Help, save, pity and defend us, O God, by your grace. *(Pause)*

13. Rejoicing in the fellowship of the Blessed Virgin Mary, of St. Joseph her spouse, of St. John the Baptist and of all the saints, let us commend ourselves, one another and our whole life to Christ our Lord.

R: To you, O Lord.

Collect: O God, whose only-begotten Son appeared in human form for our salvation, grant that we may become inwardly like him who was outwardly like us; he lives and reigns with you and the Holy Spirit, one God, for ever and ever.

All: Amen.

Blessing

1. May Jesus Christ, the Word made flesh, bless you and keep/you.

All: Amen.
2. May the Light of the world graciously smile/upon you.

All: Amen.
3. May the/Lord grant you peace.

All: Amen.

Christmas—Morning Prayer

Invitatory

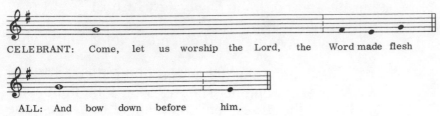

CELEBRANT: Come, let us worship the Lord, the Word made flesh

ALL: And bow down before him.

MORNING HYMN

Corde natus ex parentis, Prudentius
Tr. J. M. Neale, 1854 & Henry W.
Baker, 1859

87.87.877

Divinum Mysterium
13th century Plainsong

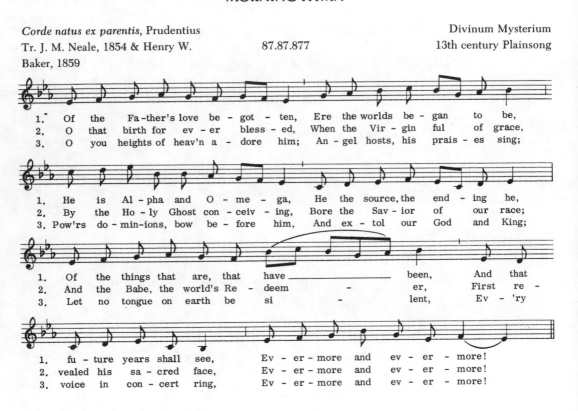

1. Of the Fa-ther's love be-got-ten, Ere the worlds be-gan to be, He is Al-pha and O-me-ga, He the source, the end-ing he, Of the things that are, that have _____ been, And that fu-ture years shall see, Ev-er-more and ev-er-more!

2. O that birth for ev-er bless-ed, When the Vir-gin ful of grace, By the Ho-ly Ghost con-ceiv-ing, Bore the Sav-ior of our race; And the Babe, the world's Re-deem ___ er, First re-vealed his sa-cred face, Ev-er-more and ev-er-more!

3. O you heights of heav'n a-dore him; An-gel hosts, his prais-es sing; Pow'rs do-min-ions, bow be-fore him, And ex-tol our God and King; Let no tongue on earth be si ___ lent, Ev-'ry voice in con-cert ring, Ev-er-more and ev-er-more!

4. Christ, to thee with God the Father,
   And, O Holy Ghost, to thee,
   Hymn and chant and high thanksgiving,
   And unwearied praises be:
   Honor, glory, and dominion,
   And eternal victory,
   Evermore and evermore!

Reading

A Reading From The Letter To The Hebrews (1:1–4): In times past, God spoke in fragmentary and varied ways to our fathers through the prophets; in this, the final age, he has spoken to us through his Son, whom he has made heir of all things and through whom he first created the universe. This Son is the reflection of the Father's glory, the exact representation of the Father's being, and he sustains all things by his powerful word. When he had cleansed us from our sins, he took his seat at the right hand of the Majesty in heaven, as far superior to the angels as the name he has inherited is superior to theirs. This is the word of the Lord.

All: Thanks be to God.

Gospel Canticle

CANTICLE OF ZECHARIAH

The Word was made flesh, al - le - lu - ia, and dwelt a - mong us, al - le - lu - ia.

Intercessions

V: Jesus, Son of God and Son of the/Virgin MAry.

R: Peace to your peo/ple on earth.

V: Jesus, hope of the penitent, our present joy and our/future REward.

V: Jesus, king most wonderful, conqueror most glorious, our consolation be/yond all TELLing.

V: Jesus, source of life, light of minds, conso/lation of all hearts.

V: Jesus, glory of the angels, dispeller of darkness,/hope of SEEKers.

V: Jesus, honey to the lips, melody to the ears, a shout of/gladness in the heart.

V: Jesus, flower of the virgin-mother, desire of mankind,/king of blessedness.

Collect: O God, who fashioned man so admirably and still more admirably repaired his fallen state, grant that we may share ever more fully in the divinity of your Son who chose to appear in our humanity; he lives and reigns with you and the Holy Spirit, one God, for ever and ever.

All: Amen.

Blessing

May the Word made flesh, the author of our salvation, bless/us and keep us.

All: A/men.

Lent—Evensong

EVENING HYMN—Weeks 1–5

Latin, 6th century
Tr. Maurice F. Bell, 1906
(Oxford U. Press)

L.M.

Melcombe
Samuel Webbe, 1782

1. The glo-ry of these for-ty days We cel-e-brate with songs of praise; For Christ, by whom all things were made, Him-self has fast-ed and has prayed.

2. A-lone and fast-ing Mos-es saw The lov-ing God who gave the law; And to E-li-jah, fast-ing, came The steeds and char-i-ots of flame.

3. So Dan-iel trained his mys-tic sight De-liv-er'd from the li-on's might; And John the Bride-groom's friend, be-came The her-ald of Mes-si-ah's name.

4. Then grant us, Lord, like them to be
   Full oft in fast and prayer with thee;
   Our spirits strengthen with thy grace,
   And give us joy to see thy face.

5. O Father, Son, and Spirit blest,
   To thee be ev'ry prayer adrest,
   Who art in threefold Name adored,
   From age to age, the only Lord.

EVENING HYMN—Holy Week

Pange lingua gloriosi
Venantius Honorius Fortunatus, 569
Tr. and adap. Rev. M. Quinn, O.P. et al.

87.87

Goldschmidt
Geistreiches Gesangbuch
Darmstadt, 1698

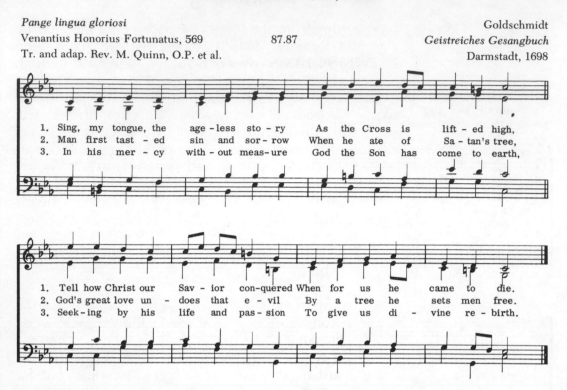

1. Sing, my tongue, the age-less sto-ry As the Cross is lift-ed high,
2. Man first tast-ed sin and sor-row When he ate of Sa-tan's tree,
3. In his mer-cy with-out meas-ure God the Son has come to earth,

1. Tell how Christ our Sav-ior con-quered When for us he came to die.
2. God's great love un-does that e-vil By a tree he sets men free.
3. Seek-ing by his life and pas-sion To give us di-vine re-birth.

4. Silence cloaks the earth and heavens
   Round the hill of Calvary;
   Fixed upon the tree of glory
   Christ endures his agony.

5. See the sign of man's redemption
   Which proclaims God's loving plan
   Christ enthroned upon a cross, has
   Liberated captive man.

6. Cross triumphant, Cross transforming
   Instrument of man's release,
   Christ's own blood from you descending
   Wins for us eternal peace.

7. Glory be to God the Father,
   Honor to his only Son,
   Reigning with the Holy Spirit,
   Persons three in God-head one.

Readings

Week 1: A reading from the letter of blessed Paul the Apostle to the Romans (1:16–17): I am not ashamed of the gospel. It is the power of God leading everyone who believes in it to salvation, the Jew first, then the Greek. For in the gospel is revealed the justice of God which begins and ends with faith; as Scripture says, "The just man shall live by faith." This is the word of the Lord.

All: Thanks be to God.

Week 2: A reading from the letter of blessed Paul the Apostle to the Romans (5:1–5): Now that we have been justified by faith, we are at peace with God through our Lord Jesus Christ. Through him we have gained access by faith to the grace in which we now stand, and we boast of our hope for the glory of God. But not only that—we even boast of our afflictions! We know that affliction makes for endurance, and endurance for tested virtue, and tested virtue for hope. And this hope will not leave us disappointed, because the love of God has been poured out in our hearts through the Holy Spirit who has been given to us. This is the word of the Lord.

All: Thanks be to God.

Week 3: A reading from the letter of blessed Paul the Apostle to the Romans (5:6–11): At the appointed time, when we were still powerless, Christ died for us godless men. It is rare that anyone should lay down his life for a just man, though it is barely possible that for a good man someone may have the courage to die. It is precisely in this that God proves his love for us: that while we were still sinners, Christ died for us. Now that we have been justified by his blood, it is all the more certain that we shall be saved by him from God's wrath. For if, when we were God's enemies, we were reconciled to him by the death of his Son, it is all the more certain that we who have been reconciled will be saved by his life. This is the word of the Lord.

All: Thanks be to God.

Week 4: A reading from the letter of blessed Paul the Apostle to the Romans (6:12–23): Do not let sin rule your mortal body and make you obey its lusts; no more shall you offer the members of your body to sin as weapons for evil. Rather, offer yourselves to God as men who have come back from the dead to life, and your bodies to God as weapons for justice. Sin will no longer have power over you; you are now under grace, not under law. . . . The wages of sin is death, but the gift of God is eternal life in Christ Jesus our Lord. This is the word of the Lord.

All: Thanks be to God.

Week 5:   A reading from the first letter of blessed Peter the Apostle (5:6–9): Bow humbly under God's mighty hand, so that in due time he may lift you high. Cast all your cares on him because he cares for you. Stay sober and alert. Your opponent the devil is prowling like a roaring lion looking for someone to devour. Resist him, solid in your faith, realizing that the brotherhood of believers is undergoing the same sufferings throughout the world. This is the word of the Lord.

All: Thanks be to God.

Holy Week: A reading from the first letter of blessed Peter the Apostle (2:21–24): Christ suffered for you and left you an example, to have you follow in his footsteps. He did no wrong; no deceit was found in his mouth. When he was insulted, he returned no insult. When he was made to suffer, he did not counter with threats. Instead, he delivered himself up to the One who judges justly. In his own body he brought your sins to the cross, so that all of us, dead to sin, could live in accord with God's will. By his wounds you were healed. This is the word of the Lord.

All: Thanks be to God.

Gospel Canticle

CANTICLE OF MARY

Week 1

The   just   man   shall   live   by   faith.

Week 2

We boast of our hope for the glo – ry of God.

Week 3

While we were still sin – ners, Christ died for us.

Week 4

The gift of God is e – ter – nal life in Christ Je – sus our Lord.

Week 5

Cast all your cares on him be – cause he cares for you.

Holy Week

By the wood of the cross joy came in – to the whole world.

Intercessions

Weeks 1–3:   1. In peace, let us pray to the Lord.

R: Lord, have mercy.

2. For peace from on high and the salvation of our souls, let us pray to the Lord.

3. For peace throughout the whole world, the welfare of the holy churches of God, and for the unity of mankind, let us pray to the Lord.

4. For all here present who await with expectation the grace of the Holy Spirit, let us pray to the Lord.

5. For those who bow their knees and hearts before the God of mercy, let us pray to the Lord.

6. For the strengthening gifts of the Holy Spirit to do all that pleases our Father, let us pray to the Lord.

7. For the blessed fruits of the Holy Spirit and the crucifixion of all self-indulgence and wicked desires, let us pray to the Lord.

8. For the grace to pray, fast and give alms as the Lord wills, let us pray to the Lord.

9. For our deliverance from all affliction, danger and sin, let us pray to the Lord.

10. Help, save, pity and defend us, O God, by your grace. *(Pause)*

11. Rejoicing in the fellowship of the Blessed Virgin Mary, of St. *Name,* and of all the saints, let us commend ourselves, one another and our whole life to Christ our Lord.

R: To you, O Lord.

Collect: Almighty God, Father of our Lord and Savior Jesus Christ, the Friend of mankind, in the beginning you created us in your own image and likeness, and when we had fallen away from this high calling and destiny, sent your only Son to redeem and restore us; by his precious and life-giving Cross, pardon our sins, deliver us from error, reform our way of living on the pattern of the Gospel and enlighten us with the radiance of the Holy Spirit; through the same Jesus Christ our Lord.

All: Amen.

Weeks 4–6: 1. In peace, let us pray to the Lord.

R: Lord, have mercy.

2. For the unity, peace and welfare of the Church of Christ, let us pray to the Lord.

3. For new brothers and sisters in the faith and unity of the one, holy, catholic and apostolic Church, let us pray to the Lord.

4. For ministers of the Gospel who speak the truth in love, let us pray to the Lord.

5. For prophets fired by God's Word and for theologians who seek God alone, let us pray to the Lord.

6. For all those who serve the needs and defend the rights of mankind, let us pray to the Lord.

7. For the destruction of demonic powers and all that lifts itself up against the Anointed Son of God, let us pray to the Lord.

8. For the elimination of slavery, exploitation and war, let us pray to the Lord.

9. For the gifts of nature and of grace we need to live full lives and serve the Gospel, let us pray to the Lord.

10. For the sick and the handicapped, the dying and the bereaved, and for the faithful departed, let us pray to the Lord.

11. Help, save, pity and defend us, O God, by your grace. *(Pause)*

12. Rejoicing in the fellowship of the Blessed Virgin Mary, of St. *Name,* and of all the saints, let us commend ourselves, one another and our whole life to Christ our Lord.

R: To you, O Lord.

Collect: Lord Jesus Christ, who descended into the womb of the Virgin and who ascended the wood of the Cross for our salvation, grant that our Lenten observances may teach us true self-denial and genuine attachment to your divine will for us; you are living and reigning with the Father and the Holy Spirit, one God, for ever and ever.

All: Amen.

Blessing

1. May Jesus Christ, the bread from heaven, bless you and keep/you.

All: Amen.

2. May the Lamb of God who laid down his life for us graciously smile/upon you.

All: Amen.

3. May the/Lord grant you peace.

All: Amen.

Lent—Morning Prayer

Invitatory

Weeks 1–5

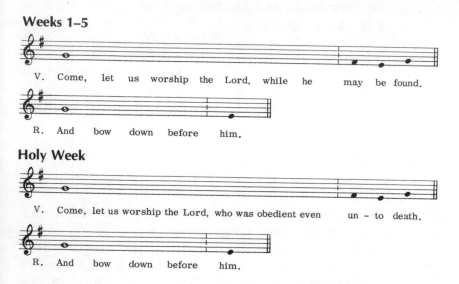

V. Come, let us worship the Lord, while he may be found.

R. And bow down before him.

Holy Week

V. Come, let us worship the Lord, who was obedient even un - to death.

R. And bow down before him.

MORNING HYMN

Jam Christe Sol Justitiae, c. 6th century
Tr. & adap. Rev. M. Quinn, O.P., et al.

L.M.

Spires
J. Klug's *Geistliche Lieder,* 1543

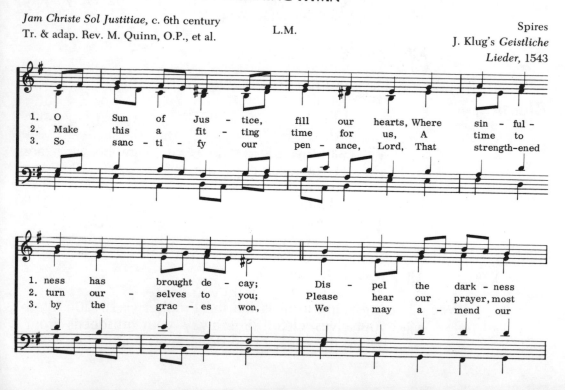

1. O Sun of Jus - tice, fill our hearts, Where sin - ful -
2. Make this a fit - ting time for us, A time to
3. So sanc - ti - fy our pen - ance, Lord, That strength-ened

1. ness has brought de - cay; Dis - pel the dark - ness
2. turn our - selves to you; Please hear our prayer, most
3. by the grac - es won, We may a - mend our

1. in our souls As now the night gives place to day.
2. pa - tient Lord, Re - pent - ance in our hearts re - new.
3. sin - ful lives And toward our goal more sure - ly run.

4. As spring awakes the frozen earth,
   So Easter blooms from Lent's restraints.
   Rejoice! for Christ will conquer death
   And bring his grace to make us saints.

5. O everlasting Trinity
   We soon shall see that day of days
   When all creation, born again,
   Will sing an Easter song of praise.

Readings

Week 1: A reading from Micah the Prophet (6:8): You have been told, O man, what is good, and what the Lord requires of you; only to do the right and to love goodness, and to walk humbly with your God. This is the word of the Lord.

All: Thanks be to God.

Week 2: A reading from Joel the Prophet (2:1–13): Blow the trumpet in Zion, sound the alarm on my holy mountain! Let all who dwell in the land tremble, for the day of the Lord is coming. . . . Yet even now, says the Lord, return to me with your whole heart, with fasting and weeping and mourning; rend your hearts and not your garments, and return to the Lord, your God. For gracious and merciful is he, slow to anger, rich in kindness, and relenting in punishment. This is the word of the Lord.

All: Thanks be to God.

Week 3: A reading from Isaiah the Prophet (1:16–20): Wash yourselves clean! Put away your misdeeds from before my eyes; cease doing evil; learn to do good.

Make justice your aim: redress the wronged, hear the orphan's plea, defend the widow. Come now, let us set things right, says the Lord: Though your sins be like scarlet, they may become white as snow; though they be crimson red, they may become white as wool. If you are willing and obey, you shall eat the good things of the land; but if you refuse and resist, the sword shall consume you: for the mouth of the Lord has spoken! This is the word of the Lord.

All: Thanks be to God.

Week 4: A reading from Ezechiel the Prophet (18:30–32): I will judge you, house of Israel, each one according to his ways, says the Lord God. Turn and be converted from all your crimes, that they may be no cause of guilt for you. Cast away from you all the crimes you have committed, and make for yourselves a new heart and a new spirit. Why should you die, O house of Israel? For I have no pleasure in the death of anyone who dies, says the Lord God. Return and live! This is the word of the Lord.

All: Thanks be to God.

Week 5: A reading from Isaiah the Prophet (55:6–9): Seek the Lord while he may be found, call him while he is near. Let the scoundrel forsake his way, and the wicked man his thoughts; let him turn to the Lord for mercy; to our God, who is generous in forgiving. For my thoughts are not your thoughts, nor are your ways my ways, says the Lord. As high as the heavens are above the earth, so high are my ways above your ways and my thoughts above your thoughts. This is the word of the Lord.

All: Thanks be to God.

Holy Week: A reading from Isaiah the Prophet (53:11–12): Through his suffering, my servant will justify many, and their guilt he shall bear. Therefore I will give him his portion among the great, and he shall divide the spoils with the mighty, because he surrendered himself to death and was counted among the wicked; and he shall take away the sins of many, and win pardon for their offenses. This is the word of the Lord.

All: Thanks be to God.

Gospel Canticle

CANTICLE OF ZECHARIAH

Week 1

Love good - ness and walk hum - bly with your God.

Week 2

Re - turn to me with your whole heart, says the Lord.

Week 3

Though your sins be like scar - let, they may be - come white as snow.

Week 4

Make for your - selves a new heart and a new spir - it.

Week 5

Seek the Lord while he may be found, call him while he is near.

Holy Week

Glo - ry to the cross of our Lord Je - sus Christ, our sal - va - tion, life and res - ur - rec - tion.

Intercessions

Weeks 1–5:

V: God of our fathers, rich in mercy and abounding/in comPASSion.

R: Hear us and have/MERcy.

V: Merciful Father, you do not desire the death of the sinner but that/he repent and live.

R: Hear us and have/MERcy.

V: Lord, change our hearts and minds during these blessed days of penance and/SORrow for sin.

R: Hear us and have/MERcy.

V: Lord, forgive us our sins as we forgive those who/sin aGAINST us.

R: Hear us and have/MERcy.

V: Lord, make us instru/ments of YOUR peace.

R: Hear us and have/MERcy.

Collect: O God, whose overflowing love for mankind is the source of our hope, mercifully regard the prayers of your penitent people; turn away your anger which we deserve for our sins, put in us a new and constant spirit and make us true followers of your Son, our Savior, Jesus Christ, who lives and reigns with you and the Holy Spirit, one God, for ever and ever.

All: Amen.

Holy Week:

V: Lord Jesus Christ, who refused to parade your e/ quality with God.

R: Good Lord, de/liver us.

V: Lord Jesus Christ, who despoiled yourself of divine privilege and accepted the/HUman condition.

R: Good Lord, de/liver us.

V: Lord Jesus Christ, who stooped even to the acceptance of death,/DEATH on a cross.

R: Good Lord, de/liver us.

V: Lord Jesus Christ, by your agony and bloody sweat, by your/cross and bitter passion.

R: Good Lord, de/liver us.

V: Lord Jesus Christ, by your glorious resurrection and ascension and by the gift/of the Holy Spirit.

R: Good Lord, de/liver us.

Collect: Almighty and everlasting God, who willed that your Son, our Savior, should become man and undergo the torment of the cross for our sake, grant that we may so walk in his suffering footsteps as to share in his victorious resurrection; through the same Jesus Christ our Lord.

All: Amen.

Blessing

May the Lord almighty order our days and deeds/in his peace.

All: A/men.

Easter—Evensong

EVENING HYMN

Ad regias agni dapes
Tr. Robert Campbell, 1849, alt.

77.77.D

Salzburg
Jakob Hintze, 1678, alt.

1. At the Lamb's high feast we sing Praise to our vic - to - rious King,
2. Where the Pas - chal blood is poured Death's dark an - gel sheathes his sword;
3. Might - y vic - tim from the sky, Hell's fierce pow'rs be - neath thee lie;

1. Who hath washed us in the tide Flow - ing from his pierc - ed side;
2. Is - rael's hosts tri - um - phant go Through the wave that drowns the foe.
3. Thou hast con - quered in the fight, Thou hast brought us life and light;

1. Praise we him, whose love di - vine Gives his sa - cred Blood for wine,
2. Praise we Christ whose blood was shed, Pas - chal vic - tim, Pas - chal bread;
3. Now no more can death ap - pall, Now no more the grave en - thrall;

1. Gives his Bod - y for the feast, Christ the vic - tim, Christ the priest.
2. With sin - cer - i - ty and love Eat we man - na from a - bove.
3. Thou hast o - pened par - a - dise, And in thee thy saints shall rise.

4. Easter triumph, Easter joy,
   Sin alone can this destroy;
   From sin's pow'r do thou set free
   Souls new-born, O Lord, in thee.
   Hymns of glory, songs of praise,
   Father, unto thee we raise:
   Risen Lord, all praise to thee
   With the Spirit ever be.

ALTERNATE EVENING HYMN

Veni, Sancte Spiritus   77.77   Aus der Tiefe
Stephen Langton, c. 1150-1228   Ascr. to Martin Herbst, 1654-81
Tr. & adap. Rev. M. Quinn, O.P., et al.   *Nurnbergisches Gesangbuch*, 1676

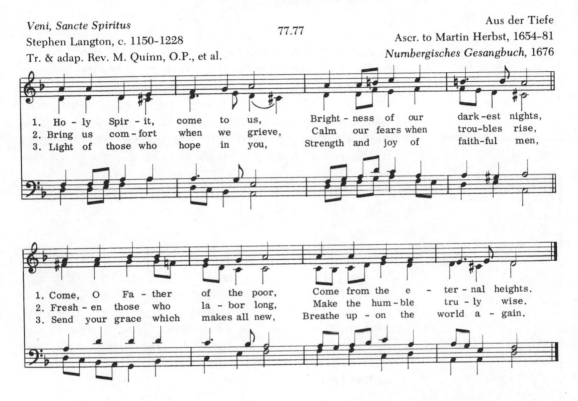

1. Ho - ly Spir - it, come to us, Bright - ness of our dark - est nights,
2. Bring us com - fort when we grieve, Calm our fears when trou - bles rise,
3. Light of those who hope in you, Strength and joy of faith - ful men,

1. Come, O Fa - ther of the poor, Come from the e - ter - nal heights.
2. Fresh - en those who la - bor long, Make the hum - ble tru - ly wise.
3. Send your grace which makes all new, Breathe up - on the world a - gain.

4. Warm with love the heart grown cold,
   Wash with grace what lies unclean,
   Heal the sick, rebuke the lax,
   Comfort men who die unseen.

5. By your seven holy gifts,
   Cleanse our sinful souls of stain,
   Lead us to our home on high
   Where in joy the blessed reign.

Readings

Week 1: A reading from the Acts of the Apostles (10:40–43): They killed Jesus, hanging him on a tree, only to have God raise him up on the third day and grant that he be seen, not by all, but only by such witnesses as had been chosen beforehand by God—by us who ate and drank with him after he rose from the dead.

He commissioned us to preach to the people and to bear witness that he is the one set apart by God as judge of the living and the dead. To him all the prophets testify, saying that everyone who believes in him has forgiveness of sins through his name. This is the word of the Lord.

All: Thanks be to God.

Week 2:   A reading from the letter of blessed Paul the Apostle to the Ephesians (4:22–24): You must lay aside your former way of life and the old self which deteriorates through illusion and desire, and acquire a fresh, spiritual way of thinking. You must put on that new man created in God's image, whose justice and holiness are born of truth. This is the word of the Lord.

All: Thanks be to God.

Week 3:   A reading from the Book of Revelation (1:17–18): When I caught sight of him I fell down at his feet as though dead. He touched me with his right hand and said: "There is nothing to fear. I am the First and the Last and the One who lives. Once I was dead but now I live—for ever and ever. I hold the keys of death and the nether world." This is the word of the Lord.

All: Thanks be to God.

Week 4:   A reading from the letter of blessed Paul the Apostle to the Ephesians (2:4–7): God is rich in mercy; because of his great love for us he brought us to life with Christ when we were dead in sin. By this favor you were saved. Both with and in Christ Jesus he raised us up and gave us a place in the heavens, that in the ages to come he might display the great wealth of his favor, manifested by his kindness to us in Christ Jesus. This is the word of the Lord.

All: Thanks be to God.

Week 5:   A reading from the first letter of blessed Paul the Apostle to the Corinthians (15:20–24): Christ is now raised from the dead, the first fruits of those who have fallen asleep. Death came through a man; hence the resurrection of the dead comes through a man also. Just as in Adam all die, so in Christ all will come to life again, but each one in proper order; Christ the first fruits and then, at his coming, all those who belong to him. After that will come the end, when, after having destroyed every sovereignty, authority, and power, he will hand over the kingdom to God the Father. This is the word of the Lord.

All: Thanks be to God.

Week 6:   A reading from the second letter of blessed Paul the Apostle to the Corinthians (4:13–15): We have that spirit of faith of which the Scripture says, "Because I believed, I spoke out." We believe and so we speak, knowing that he who raised up the Lord Jesus will raise us up along with Jesus and place both us and you in his presence. Indeed, everything is ordered to your benefit, so that the grace bestowed in abundance may bring greater glory to God because those who give thanks are many. This is the word of the Lord.

All: Thanks be to God.

Week 7:   A reading from the first letter of blessed Peter the Apostle (3:18–22): The reason why Christ died for sins once for all, the just man for the sake of the unjust, was that he might lead you to God. He was put to death insofar as fleshly existence goes, but was given life in the realm of the spirit. . . . He went to heaven and is at God's right hand, with angelic rulers and powers subjected to him. This is the word of the Lord.

All: Thanks be to God.

Gospel Canticle

CANTICLE OF MARY

Week 1

This is the day the Lord has made, let us re-joice and be glad, al-le-lu-ia.

Week 2

All you who have been bap-tized in-to Christ have put on Christ, al-le-lu-ia.

Week 3

The Lord has ris-en and has ap-peared to Pe-ter, al-le-lu-ia.

Week 4

The dis-ci-ples rec-og-nized the Lord Je-sus in the break-ing of bread, al-le-lu-ia.

Week 5

This is my com-mand-ment Love one an-oth-er as I have loved you, al-le-lu-ia.

Week 6

I am leav-ing the world and go-ing

to the Fa - ther, al - le - lu - ia.

Week 7

Send out your Spir - it and re - new the

face of the earth al - le - lu - ia.

Intercessions

1. In the peace of the Risen Christ, let us pray to the Lord.

R: Lord, have mercy.

2. For peace from on high and for the salvation of our souls, let us pray to the Lord.

3. That the Lord Jesus Christ, our Savior, may grant us victory over the temptations of our visible and invisible enemies, let us pray to the Lord.

4. That he may crush beneath our feet the Prince of Darkness and his powers, let us pray to the Lord.

5. That he may raise us up with him and make us rise from the tomb of our sins and offenses, let us pray to the Lord.

6. That he may fill us with the joy and happiness of his holy and life-giving resurrection, let us pray to the Lord.

7. That we may enter the chamber of his divine wedding-feast and rejoice without limit together with the hosts of saints in the Church Triumphant, let us pray to the Lord.

8. Help, save, pity and defend us, O God, by your grace. *(Pause)*

9. Rejoicing in the fellowship of the Blessed Virgin Mary, of St. *Name,* and of all the saints, let us commend ourselves, one another and our whole life to Christ our Lord.

R: To you, O Lord.

Collect: O Risen Lord, whose power is beyond compare and whose love for mankind is beyond words to describe, in your compassion hear the prayer of your ransomed people and grant us the riches of your mercy as you have promised; for you are our Light and our Resurrection, O Christ our Lord, and we glorify you and your eternal Father and your Holy and life-giving Spirit, now and for ever.

All: Amen.

Or: O God of salvation, who heard your Son when he cried to you from the midst of his foes and raised him up out of the sleep of death, uphold your people, shield us from our enemies and bring us home in safety to your holy mountain; through the same Jesus Christ our Lord.

All: Amen.

Or: O God, on the first Pentecost you instructed the hearts of those who believed in you by the light of the Holy Spirit; under the inspiration of the same Spirit, give us a taste for what is right and true and a continuing sense of his joy-bringing presence and power; through Jesus Christ our Lord.

All: Amen.

Blessing

1. May Jesus Christ, who was put to death for our sins, bless you and/keep you.

All: Amen.
2. May he who was raised to life for our justification graciously smile/upon you.

All: Amen.
3. May Christ, our victorious King,/grant you peace.

All: Amen.

Easter—Morning Prayer

Invitatory

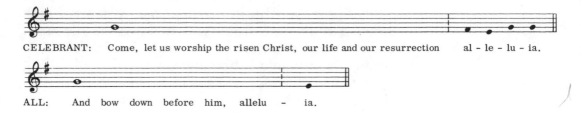

CELEBRANT: Come, let us worship the risen Christ, our life and our resurrection al - le - lu - ia.

ALL: And bow down before him, allelu - ia.

MORNING HYMN

Aurora Lucis rutilat, c. 8th cent.
Tr. & adap. Rev. M. Quin, O.P., et al

C.M.

St. Magnus
Jeremiah Clark, c. 1670-1707
Playford's *The Divine Companion*, 1707

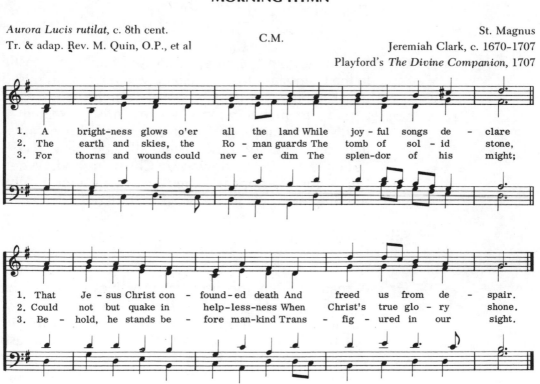

1. A bright-ness glows o'er all the land While joy - ful songs de - clare
2. The earth and skies, the Ro - man guards The tomb of sol - id stone,
3. For thorns and wounds could nev - er dim The splen-dor of his might;

1. That Je - sus Christ con - found-ed death And freed us from de - spair.
2. Could not but quake in help-less-ness When Christ's true glo - ry shone.
3. Be - hold, he stands be - fore man-kind Trans - fig - ured in our sight.

4. His followers were sorrowful,
Confused and filled with dread,
Until they saw their risen Lord,
The first-born of the dead.

5. We beg you now, O risen Lord,
Direct your faithful friends,
Defend us all from Satan's schemes
Receive us when life ends.

Readings

A reading from the letter of blessed Peter the Apostle (1:3–5): Praised be the God and Father of our Lord Jesus Christ, he who in his great mercy gave us new birth; a birth unto hope which draws its life from the resurrection of Jesus Christ from the dead; a birth to an imperishable inheritance, incapable of fading or defilement, which is kept in heaven for you who are guarded with God's power through faith; a birth to a salvation which stands ready to be revealed in the last days. This is the word of the Lord.

All: Thanks be to God.

Or: A reading from the letter of blessed Paul the Apostle to the Colossians (3:1–4): Since you have been raised up in company with Christ, set your heart on what pertains to higher realms where Christ is seated at God's right hand. Be intent on things above rather than on things of earth. After all, you have died! Your life is hidden now with Christ in God. When Christ our life appears, then you shall appear with him in glory. This is the word of the Lord.

All: Thanks be to God.

Or: A reading from the first letter of blessed Paul the Apostle to the Corinthians (5:6–8): Do you not know that a little yeast has its effect all through the dough? Get rid of the old yeast to make of yourselves fresh dough, unleavened loaves, as it were; Christ our Passover has been sacrificed. Let us celebrate the feast not with the old yeast, that of corruption and wickedness, but with the unleavened bread of sincerity and truth. This is the word of the Lord.

All: Thanks be to God.

Gospel Canticle

CANTICLE OF ZECHARIAH

Week 1

This is the day the Lord has made, let us re- joice and be glad, al - le - lu - ia.

Week 2

The Mes - si - ah must suf - fer and rise from the dead on the third day, al - le - lu - ia.

Week 3

Look at my hands and my feet; it is real - ly I, al - le - lu - ia.

Week 4

Once ris - en from the dead, Christ will nev - er die a - gain, al - le - lu - ia.

Week 5

Christ is seat - ed at God's right hand, al - le - lu - ia.

Week 6

I am as - cen - ding to my Fa - ther and your Fa - ther, to my God and your God! al - le - lu - ia.

Week 7

Come, Ho - ly Spir - it, fill the hearts of your faith - ful, al - le - lu - ia.

Intercessions

V: Lord Jesus Christ, who died for our sins and/rose for our salvation.

R: Hear us,/Risen Lord.

V: Lord Jesus Christ, who conquered death by death and gave life to/THOSE in the graves.

R: Hear us,/Risen Lord.

V: Lord Jesus Christ, who overcame death's sting, and gave fresh life/to our fallen world.

R: Hear us,/Risen Lord.

V: Lord Jesus Christ, who established the new and eternal covenant/in your precious blood.

R: Hear us,/Risen Lord.

V: Lord Jesus Christ, who set us free from the/law of sin and death.

R: Hear us,/Risen Lord.

V: Lord Jesus Christ, pleading for us at/GOD'S RIGHT hand.

R: Hear us,/Risen Lord.

V: Lord Jesus Christ, the same yesterday, to/DAY and for ever.

R: Hear us,/Risen Lord.

Collect: Heavenly Father, when Christ our Paschal Lamb was sacrificed he overcame death by his own dying and restored us to life by his own rising; in virtue of his life-giving Passover, pour your Holy Spirit into our hearts, fill us with awe and reverence for you and with love and compassion for our neighbor; through the same Jesus Christ our Lord.

All: Amen.

Or: O God, who for our redemption delivered up your only-begotten Son to the death of the cross and by his glorious resurrection rescued us from the power of the enemy; help us to die daily to sin that we may always live with him in the power and the glory of his risen life; through the same Jesus Christ our Lord.

All: Amen.

Or: O Shepherd of Israel, you rescued your Son, our Savior, from the death-dark valley and anointed him as Messiah and Lord; grant that we may drink from the over-flowing cup of his Spirit and dwell in your house all the days of our life; through the same Jesus Christ our Lord.

All: Amen.

Blessing

Assistant: The Lord is risen,/alleluia.

All: He has risen, indeed, allelui/a.

Celebrant: May the peace and mercy of the risen Christ rest/on us all.

All: A/men.

The Common of Saints

"In celebrating this annual cycle of Christ's mysteries, holy Church honors with especial love the Blessed Mary, Mother of God, who is joined by an inseparable bond to the saving work of her Son. In her the Church holds up and admires the most excellent fruit of the redemption, and joyfully contemplates, as in a faultless image, that which she herself desires and hopes wholly to be.

The Church has also included in the annual cycle days devoted to the memory of the martyrs and other saints. Raised up to perfection by the manifold grace of God, and already in possession of eternal salvation, they sing God's perfect praise in heaven and offer prayers for us. By celebrating the passage of these saints from earth to heaven the Church proclaims the paschal mystery achieved in the saints who have suffered and been glorified with Christ; she proposes them to the faithful as examples drawing all to the Father through Christ, and through their merits she pleads for God's favors."

The Constitution on the Sacred Liturgy, 103–104

Common of The Blessed Virgin Mary—
Morning Prayer

Invitatory

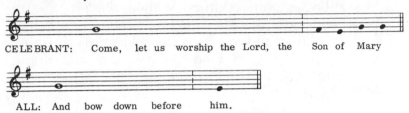

CELEBRANT: Come, let us worship the Lord, the Son of Mary

ALL: And bow down before him.

MORNING HYMN

Ave Maris Stella, c. 9th cent.
Tr. & adap. Rev. M. Quinn, O.P., et al

77.77

Gott sei dank
Freylinghausen's *Gesangbuch,* 1704

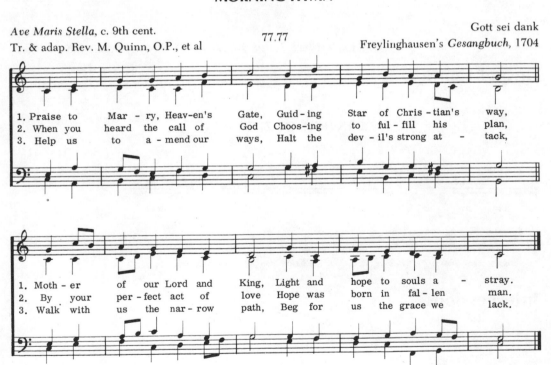

1. Praise to Mar - ry, Heav-en's Gate, Guid - ing Star of Chris - tian's way,
2. When you heard the call of God Choos-ing to ful - fill his plan,
3. Help us to a - mend our ways, Halt the dev - il's strong at - tack,

1. Moth - er of our Lord and King, Light and hope to souls a - stray.
2. By your per - fect act of love Hope was born in fal - len man.
3. Walk with us the nar - row path, Beg for us the grace we lack.

4. Mary, show your motherhood,
   Bring your children's prayers to Christ
   Christ, your son, who ransomed man,
   Who, for us, was sacrificed.

5. Virgin chosen, singly blest,
   Ever faithful to God's call
   Guide us in this earthly life,
   Guard us lest, deceived, we fall.

6. Mary, help us live our faith
   So that we may see your son;
   Join our humble prayers to yours,
   Till life's ceaseless war is won.

7. Praise the Father, praise the Son,
   Praise the holy Paraclete;
   Offer all through Mary's hands,
   Let her make our prayers complete.

Reading

A reading from the book of the prophet Isaiah (61:10–11): I rejoice heartily in the Lord, in my God is the joy of my soul; for he has clothed me with a robe of salvation, and wrapped me in a mantle of justice, like a bridegroom adorned with a diadem, like a bride bedecked with her jewels. As the earth brings forth its plants, and a garden makes its growth spring up, so will the Lord God make justice and praise spring up before all the nations. This is the word of the Lord.

All: Thanks be to God.

Other selections: Judith 13:17, 18-20; Song of Songs 2:8-14

Gospel Canticle

CANTICLE OF ZECHARIAH

Blest are you, O Virgin Mary, of you was born the Sun of justice, Christ our God.

Intercessions

1. Lord Jesus Christ, Son of God and Son of the/ Blessed Virgin Mary.

All: Hear us/and have mercy.

2. Lord Jesus Christ, who prepared the body and soul of the immaculate virgin to/be your MOther.

3. Lord Jesus Christ, who willed that your holy mother be praised in/every generation.

4. Lord Jesus Christ, who lived in subjection in the home of/MAry and Joseph.

5. Lord Jesus Christ, who had Mary standing at the/FOOT of your cross.

6. Lord Jesus Christ, who lifted up the lowly virgin to share in your/HEAvenly kingdom.

7. Lord Jesus Christ, who crowned your blessed mother as/queen of HEAven.

Collect: Almighty and everlasting God, who by the cooperation of the Holy Spirit prepared the body and soul of the glorious virgin-mother Mary to be a fit dwelling for your Son, grant that we who rejoice in her memory may be freed by her kindly intercession both·from present ills and from eternal death; through the same Christ our Lord.

All: Amen.

Blessing

May Jesus, Son of Mary, grant us par/don and peace.

All: A/men.

Common of The Blessed Virgin Mary— Evensong

EVENING HYMN

Quem terra, pontus, sidera
Venantius Fortunatus, 530–605
Tr. J. M. Neale, 1818–1866

L.M.

Eisenach
From a melody by
J. H. Shein, 1586–1630

1. The God whom earth and sea and sky A - dore and
2. The God whose will by moon and sun And all things
3. How blest that Moth - er, in whose shrine The Mak - er

1. praise and mag - ni - fy, Who o - ver all cre -
2. in due course is done, Is borne up - on a
3. of the world di - vine, Whose hand con - tains the

1. a - tion reigns, The Vir - gin's spot - less womb con - tains.
2. Maid - en's breast Of full - est heav'n-ly grace pos - sessed.
3. earth and sky Vouch - safed, as in his ark, to lie!

4. Blest in the message Gabriel brought;
Blest by the work the Spirit wrought:
From whom the great Desire of earth
Took human flesh and human birth.

5. All honor, praise, and glory be,
O Jesus, Virgin-born, to thee!
All glory, as is ever meet,
To Father and to Paraclete.

Reading

A reading from the letter of blessed Paul the Apostle to the Galatians (4:3–7): While we were not yet of age, we were like slaves subordinated to the elements of the world; but when the designated time had come, God sent forth his Son born of a woman, born under the law, to deliver from the law those who were subjected to it, so that we might receive our status as adopted sons. The proof that you are sons is the fact that God has sent forth into our hearts the spirit of his Son which cries out "Abba!" ("Father") You are no longer a slave but a son! And the fact that you are a son makes you an heir, by God's design. This is the word of the Lord.

All: Thanks be to God.

Other selections: Sirach 24:2-12; 24:13-22; Isaiah 62:1-5; Rev 12:1-18

Gospel Canticle

CANTICLE OF MARY

Blest are you a - mong wom - en and blest is the fruit of your womb.

Intercessions

1. With holy Mary, daughter of God the Father, mother of God the Son and bride of the Spirit, let us pray to the Lord.

All: Lord, have mercy.

2. With holy Mary, child of our father Abraham and mother of the Messiah, let us pray to the Lord.
3. With holy Mary, blossoming rod of Jesse and fruit of David's line, let us pray to the Lord.

4. With holy Mary, who enclosed in her womb him whom the whole world cannot contain, let us pray to the Lord.
5. With holy Mary, who brought forth God and man, reconciling the highest and the lowest, let us pray to the Lord.
6. With holy Mary, who heard the Word of God and kept it, let us pray to the Lord.
7. With holy Mary, mother of Christians and helper of the afflicted, let us pray to the Lord.
8. Help, save, pity and defend us, O God, by your grace. *(Pause)*
9. Rejoicing in the fellowship of the Blessed Virgin Mary and of all the saints, let us commend ourselves, one another, and our whole life to Christ our Lord.

All: To you, O Lord.

Collect: Almighty and everlasting God, who willed that your Word should take flesh in the womb of the blessed Virgin Mary by the power of your overshadowing Spirit, by her affectionate intercession deliver us from all present sin and sorrow, and conduct us to the everlasting joys of our heavenly home; through the same Jesus Christ our Lord.

All: Amen.

Blessing

1. May Christ, our true God, born of the Virgin, bless you and keep/you.

All: Amen.
2. May the designated Son and Heir graciously smile/upon you.

All: Amen.
3. May the/Lord grant you peace.

All: Amen.

Common of Apostles and Evangelists—Morning Prayer

Invitatory

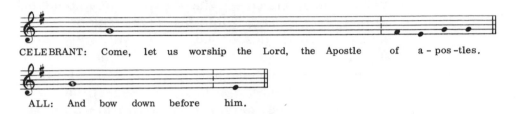

CELEBRANT: Come, let us worship the Lord, the Apostle of a-pos-tles.

ALL: And bow down before him.

MORNING HYMN

Based on *Te Deum laudamus*
Tate and Brady's *Supplement*
to the New Version. . . . 1700, alt.

C.M.

St. Peter
A. R. Reinagle, 1799–1877

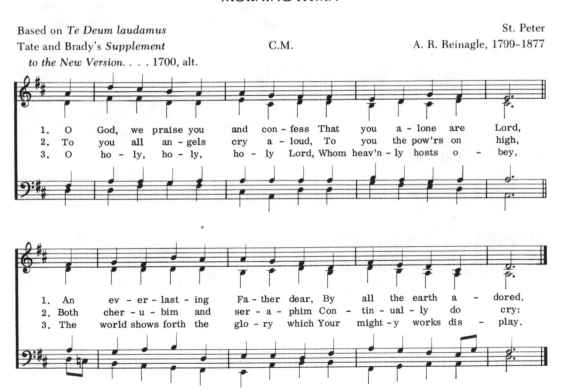

1. O God, we praise you and con-fess That you a-lone are Lord,
2. To you all an-gels cry a-loud, To you the pow'rs on high,
3. O ho-ly, ho-ly, ho-ly Lord, Whom heav'n-ly hosts o-bey,

1. An ev-er-last-ing Fa-ther dear, By all the earth a-dored.
2. Both cher-u-bim and ser-a-phim Con-tin-ual-ly do cry:
3. The world shows forth the glo-ry which Your might-y works dis-play.

4. Th'apostles glorious company,
   And prophets crowned with light,
   With all the martyrs, noble host,
   Your constant praise recite.

5. The holy Church throughout the world
   Confesses Christ as Lord,
   The boundless Father's majesty,
   The Paraclete adored.

Reading

A reading from blessed Paul the Apostle to the Ephesians (4:7–13): Each of us has received God's favor in the measure in which Christ bestows it. Thus you find Scripture saying: "When he ascended on high, he took a host of captives and gave gifts to men." "He ascended"—what does this mean but that he had first descended into the lower regions of the earth? He who descended is the very one who ascended high above the heavens, that he might fill all men with his gifts. It is he who gave apostles, prophets, evangelists, pastors and teachers in roles of service for the faithful to build up the body of Christ, till we become one in faith and in the knowledge of God's Son, and form that perfect man who is Christ come to fill stature. This is the word of the Lord.

All: Thanks be to God.

Other selections: 1 Cor 1:18-2:5; 4:1-16; 9:1-23

Gospel Canticle

CANTICLE OF ZECHARIAH

You are to be my wit-ness-es e-ven to the ends of the earth.

Intercessions

Collect: God our Father, by the power of your Holy Spirit the chosen apostles of your Son bore witness to his blessed death and resurrection; grant that we may follow their example and be, in our turn, faithful witnesses to the truth of the gospel; through the same Jesus Christ our Lord.

All: Amen.

Blessing

May our Lord Jesus Christ, the King of Apostles, bless / you and keep you.

All: A / men.

Common of Apostles and Evangelists—Evensong

EVENING HYMN

Samuel John Stone, 1866, alt.   76.76.D   Aurelia
                                                         Samuel Sebastian Wesley, 1864

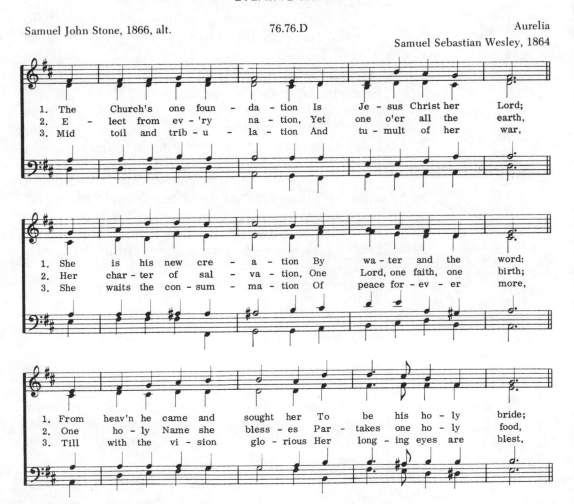

1. The Church's one foun — da — tion Is Je - sus Christ her Lord;
2. E - lect from ev - 'ry na - tion, Yet one o'er all the earth,
3. Mid toil and trib - u — la - tion And tu - mult of her war,

1. She is his new cre — a - tion By wa - ter and the word:
2. Her char - ter of sal — va - tion, One Lord, one faith, one birth;
3. She waits the con - sum — ma - tion Of peace for - ev - er more,

1. From heav'n he came and sought her To be his ho - ly bride;
2. One ho - ly Name she bless - es Par - takes one ho - ly food,
3. Till with the vi - sion glo - rious Her long - ing eyes are blest,

1. With   his   own blood   he   bought   her, And   for   her   life   he   died.
2. And   to   one hope   she   press - es, With   ev - 'ry grace   en - dued.
3. And   the   great Church vic - to - rious Shall   be   the Church   at   rest.

4. Yet she on earth hath union
    With God, the Three in One,
    And ever holds communion
    With those whose rest is won.
    O happy ones and holy!
    Lord, give us grace that we
    Like them, the meek and lowly,
    On high may dwell with thee.

Reading

A reading from the Acts of the Apostles (4:32–35): The community of believers were of one heart and one mind. None of them ever claimed anything as his own; rather, everything was held in common. With power the apostles bore witness to the resurrection of the Lord Jesus, and great respect was paid to them all; nor was there anyone needy among them, for all who owned property or houses sold them and donated the proceeds. They used to lay them at the feet of the apostles to be distributed to everyone according to his need. This is the word of the Lord.

All: Thanks be to God.

Other selections: Acts 2:42-45; 5:12-32; 10:34-43

Gospel Canticle

CANTICLE OF MARY

Go   and make   dis - ci - ples   of   all   na -   tions.

Intercessions

1. In peace, let us pray to the Lord.

All: Lord, have mercy.

2. With the great Mother of God, Mary most holy, the queen of apostles, let us pray to the Lord.

3. With the glorious choir of apostles chosen by Christ, let us pray to the Lord.

4. With the blessed apostles and martyrs, Peter and Paul, who made disciples of all nations, let us pray to the Lord.

5. With all the holy apostles, the salt of the earth and the light of the world, let us pray to the Lord.

6. For the preservation of the catholic faith that comes to us from the apostles, let us pray to the Lord.

7. For the missionary apostolate of the Church even to the ends of the earth, let us pray to the Lord.

8. For apostles, prophets, evangelists, pastors and teachers to serve the faithful and build up the body of Christ, let us pray to the Lord.

9. For the preaching of sound and apostolic doctrine, in season and out of season, let us pray to the Lord.

10. For the wise and courageous use of the keys of the kingdom in binding and loosing, let us pray to the Lord.

11. For the unity of all Christians in the one, holy, catholic and apostolic Church, let us pray to the Lord.

12. Help, save, pity and defend us, O God, by your grace. *(Pause)*

13. Rejoicing in the fellowship of the Blessed Virgin Mary, of the holy apostle (and evangelist), *Name,* and of all the saints, let us commend ourselves, one another, and our whole life to Christ our Lord.

All: To you, O Lord.

Collect: Heavenly Father, your Son commissioned his chosen apostles to preach the good news to all creation; strengthen us with apostolic teaching and empower us to be your faithful witnesses in the world; through the same Jesus Christ our Lord.

All: Amen.

Blessing

1. May Christ, the King of the apostles, bless you and keep/you.

All: Amen.
2. May the Author of the true faith graciously smile/upon you.

All: Amen.
3. May the/Lord grant you peace.

All: Amen.

Common of Martyrs—Morning Prayer

Invitatory

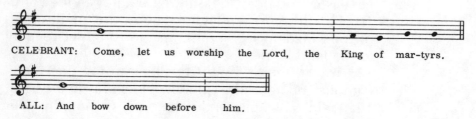

CELEBRANT: Come, let us worship the Lord, the King of mar-tyrs.

ALL: And bow down before him.

MORNING HYMN

Isaac Watts, 1707

C.M.

St. Flavian
Day's Psalter, 1563

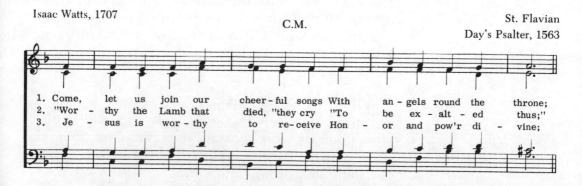

1. Come, let us join our cheer-ful songs With an - gels round the throne;
2. "Wor - thy the Lamb that died," they cry "To be ex - alt - ed thus;"
3. Je - sus is wor - thy to re-ceive Hon - or and pow'r di - vine;

1. Ten thou-sand thou-sand are their tongues, But all their joys are one.
2. "Wor - thy the Lamb," our lips re - ply, "For he was slain for us."
3. And bless-ings, more than we can give, Be, Lord, for ev - er thine.

4. Let all creation join in one
   To bless the sacred Name
   Of him that sits upon the throne,
   And to adore the Lamb.

Reading

A reading from the second letter of blessed Paul the Apostle to the Corinthians (1:3–7): Praised be God, the Father of our Lord Jesus Christ, the Father of mercies, and the God of all consolation! He comforts us in all our afflictions and thus enables us to comfort those who are in trouble, with the same consolation we have received from him. As we have shared much in the suffering of Christ, so through Christ do we share abundantly in his consolation. If we are afflicted it is for your encouragement and salvation, and when we are consoled it is for your consolation, so that you may endure patiently the same sufferings we endure. Our hope for you is firm because we know that just as you share in the sufferings, so you will share in the consolation. This is the word of the Lord.

All: Thanks be to God.

Other selections: Wis 3:1-9; 4:7-18; Sirach 51:1-17

Gospel Canticle

CANTICLE OF ZECHARIAH

They have washed their robes and made them white in the blood of the Lamb.

Intercessions

Collect: Lord our God, strength of the martyrs who shed their blood for Christ, help us by their prayers to live faithfully and to endure all testing; through the same Christ our Lord.

All: Amen.

Blessing

May our Lord Jesus Christ, the King of martyrs, bless/you and keep you.

All: A/men.

Common of Martyrs—Evensong

EVENING HYMN

Edward Perronet, 1779 and 1780
Alt. John Rippon

C.M.

Coronation
Oliver Holden, 1792

1. All hail the power of Je - sus' name! Let an - gels pros - trate fall; Bring forth the roy - al di - a - dem,
2. Ye cho - sen seed of Is - rael's race, Ye ran-somed of the fall, Hail Him who saves you by His grace,
3. Let ev - ery kin - dred, ev - ery tribe, On this ter - res - trial ball, To Him all maj - es - ty as - cribe,

1. And crown Him Lord of all; Bring forth the roy - al
2. And crown Him Lord of all; Hail Him who saves you
3. And crown Him Lord of all; To Him all maj - es -

1. di - a - dem, And crown Him Lord of all!
2. by His grace, And crown Him Lord of all!
3. ty as cribe, And crown Him Lord of all!

4. O that with yonder sacred throng
We at His feet may fall!
We'll join the everlasting song,
And crown Him Lord of all ;
We'll join the everlasting song,
And crown Him Lord of all.

Reading

A reading from the first letter of blessed Peter the Apostle (4:12–17): Do not be surprised, beloved, that a trial by fire is occurring in your midst. It is a test for you, but it should not catch you off guard. Rejoice instead, in the measure that you share Christ's sufferings. When his glory is revealed, you will rejoice exultantly. Happy are you when you are insulted for the sake of Christ, for then God's Spirit in its glory has come to rest on you. See to it that none of you suffers for being a murderer, a thief, a malefactor, or a destroyer of another's rights. If anyone suffers for being a Christian, however, he ought not to be ashamed. He should rather glorify God in virtue of that name. The season of judgment has begun, and begun with God's own household. This is the word of the Lord.

All: Thanks be to God.

Other selections: Rom 8:14-39; Heb 11:33-12:4; Rev 3:7-13; 6:9-11; 7:9-17; 20:4-6

Gospel Canticle

CANTICLE OF MARY

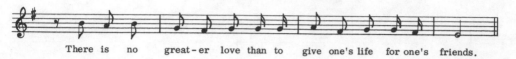

There is no great-er love than to give one's life for one's friends.

Intercessions

1. In peace, let us pray to the Lord.

All: Lord, have mercy.

2. By the power of the life-giving cross sprinkled with the priceless blood of Christ, let us pray to the Lord.

3. With the great Mother of God, Mary most holy, the queen of martyrs, let us pray to the Lord.

4. With John the Baptist, beheaded by Herod, and with Stephen the Protomartyr, who forgave his executioners, let us pray to the Lord.

5. With Peter the Shepherd, who ascended the cross, and Paul, the Apostle to the Gentiles, who gave his neck to the sword, let us pray to the Lord.

6. With St. *Name,* who gave up his (her, their) life for Christ's sake, let us pray to the Lord.

7. For the grace to glory in the cross of persecution, let us pray to the Lord.

8. For our persecuted brethren and for all who suffer for the sake of conscience, let us pray to the Lord.

9. For our deliverance from all sin and fear of death, let us pray to the Lord.

10. Help, save, pity and defend us, O God, by your grace. *(Pause)*

11. Rejoicing in the fellowship of the Blessed Virgin Mary and of all the saints, let us commend ourselves, one another, and our whole life to Christ our Lord.

All: To you, O Lord.

Collect: Heavenly Father, may the steadfast witness of the noble army of martyrs deliver us from fear and make us stronger in our love for you; through Christ our Lord.

All: Amen.

Blessing

1. May Christ, the King of martyrs, bless you and keep/you.

All: Amen.
2. May he who triumphs over death graciously smile/upon you.

All: Amen.
3. May the/Lord grant you peace.

All: Amen.

Common of Holy Men and Women— Morning Prayer

Invitatory

Come, let us worship the Lord, the King of all saints.

And bow down before him.

MORNING HYMN

Leonard Bacon, 1823

77.77.D

St. George's Windsor
George Job Elvey, 1858

1. Wake the song of ju-bi-lee, Let it ech-o o'er the sea!
2. Now the des-ert lands re-joice, And the is-lands join their voice,
3. Bless-ing, hon-or, glo-ry, might, Are the con-q'ror's na-tive right;

1. Now is come the prom-ised hour, Je-sus reigns with sov'-reign pow'r.
2. Yes, the whole cre-a-tion sings, "Je-sus is the King of kings."
3. Thrones and pow'rs be-fore him fall, Lamb of God and Lord of all.

1. All ye na-tions, join and sing, Christ of lords and kings is King
2. See the ran-som'd mil-lions stand, Palms of con-quest in their hands,
3. Time has near-ly reached its sum; All things with the bride say "come,"

1. Let it sound from shore to shore Je-sus reigns for-ev-er-more.
2. This be-fore the throne their strain, Hell is van-quished, death is slain.
3. Je-sus, whom all worlds a-dore, Come, and reign for-ev-er-more.

ALTERNATE MORNING HYMN

Charles Wesley, 1759

C.M.

Dundee

Scottish Psalter, 1615

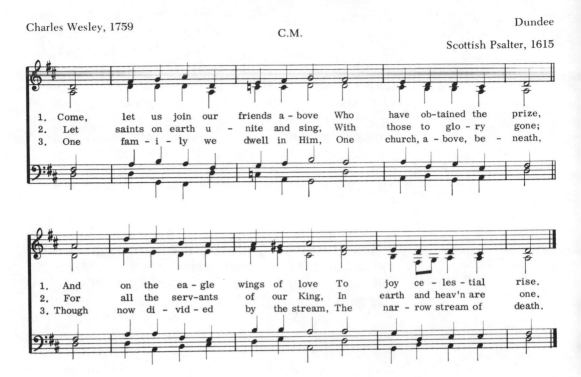

1. Come, let us join our friends a - bove Who have ob-tained the prize,
2. Let saints on earth u - nite and sing, With those to glo - ry gone;
3. One fam - i - ly we dwell in Him, One church, a - bove, be - neath,

1. And on the ea - gle wings of love To joy ce - les - tial rise.
2. For all the serv-ants of our King, In earth and heav'n are one.
3. Though now di - vid - ed by the stream, The nar - row stream of death.

4. One army of the living God,
   To His command we bow;
   Part of His host have crossed the flood
   And part are crossing now.

5. E'en now by faith we join our hands
   With those that went before,
   And greet the blood redeemed bands
   On the eternal shore.

Readings

1. Pastors: A reading from the first letter of blessed Peter the Apostle (5:1–4): To the elders among you I, a fellow elder, a witness of Christ's sufferings and sharer in the glory that is to be revealed, make this appeal. God's flock is in your midst; give it a shepherd's care. Watch over it willingly as God would have you do, not under constraint, and not for shameful profit either, but generously. Be examples to the flock, not lording it over those assigned to you, so that when the chief Shepherd appears you will win for yourselves the unfading crown of glory. This is the word of the Lord.

All: Thanks be to God.

2. Saints: A reading from the letter of blessed Paul the Apostle to the Philippians (4:8–9): Your thoughts should be wholly directed to all that is true, all that deserves respect, all that is honest, pure, admirable, decent, virtuous, or worthy of praise. Live according to what you have learned and accepted, what you have heard me say and seen me do. Then will the God of peace be with you. This is the word of the Lord.

All: Thanks be to God.

Or: A reading from the letter of blessed Paul the Apostle to the Colossians (1:9–14): We have been praying for you unceasingly and asking that you may attain full knowledge of his will through perfect wisdom and spiritual insight. Then you will lead a life worthy of the Lord and pleasing to him in every way. You will multiply good works of every sort and grow in the knowledge of God. By the might of his glory you will be endowed with the strength needed to stand fast, even to endure joyfully whatever may come, giving thanks to the Father for having made you worthy to share the lot of the saints in light. He rescued us from the power of darkness and brought us into the kingdom of his beloved Son. Through him we have redemption, the forgiveness of our sins. This is the word of the Lord.

All: Thanks be to God.

Gospel Canticle

CANTICLE OF ZECHARIAH

1. Pastors

The good shep - herd lays down his life for the sheep

2. Saints

He who be lieves in me has e - ter - nal life.

Or:

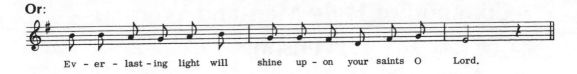

Ev - er - last - ing light will shine up - on your saints O Lord.

Intercessions

Collects—

1. Pastors: Almighty and everlasting God, you have established our Lord Jesus Christ as the high priest of the good things to come; by his power raise up zealous pastors for your faithful people, and by the example of our fathers in the faith teach them to give their lives for the good of the flock; through the same Jesus Christ our Lord.

All: Amen.

2. Saints: Gracious Father, as we call to mind the sacred memory of blessed *Name,* your faithful servant, we ask that we may believe in you more fully and serve you more fervently to the honor and glory of your name; through Jesus Christ our Lord.

All: Amen.

Or: O God, by your grace we live in communion with all your saints; by their prayers make us true disciples of your Son during our earthly pilgrimage and in our heavenly home let us share their fullness of joy; through Jesus Christ our Lord.

All: Amen.

Blessing

May our Lord Jesus Christ, the King of all saints, bless/you and keep you.

All: A/men.

Common of Holy Men and Women—
Evensong

EVENING HYMN

Caroline Maria Noel, 1875

65.65.D

King's Weston
Ralph Vaughan Williams, 1925
Arr. for *The Hymnbook;* 1955

1. At the name of Je - sus Ev - 'ry knee shall bow,
2. At His voice cre - a - tion Sprang at once to sight,
3. Hum-bled for a sea - son, To re-ceive a name

1. Ev 'ry tongue con - fess Him King of glo - ry now;
2. All the an - gel fac - es All the hosts of light,
3. From the lips of sin - ners Un - to whom He came,

1. "Tis the Fa - ther's plea - sure We should call Him Lord,
2. Thrones and dom - i - na - tions Stars up - on their way,
3. Faith-ful - ly He bore it Spot-less to the last,

1. Who from the be - gin - ning Was the might - y Word.
2. All the heav'n - ly or - ders, In their great ar - ray.
3. Brought it back vic - to - rious, When from death He passed;

4. In your hearts enthrone Him;
There let Him subdue
All that is not holy,
All that is not true:
Crown him as your Captain
In temptation's hour;
Let His will enfold you
In its light and power.

5. Brothers, this Lord Jesus
Shall return again,
With His Father's glory,
With His angel train;
For all wreathes of empire
Meet upon His brow,
And our hearts confess Him
King of glory now.

ALTERNATE EVENING HYMN

Thomas Kelly, 1820

C.M.

St. Magnus
Jeremiah Clark, c. 1670–1707
Playford's *The Divine Companion*, 1707

1. The head that once was crowned with thorns Is crowned with glo - ry now;
2. The high-est place that heav'n af-fords Is his, is his by right,
3. The joy of all who dwell a - bove The joy of all be - low,

1. A roy - al di - a - dem a-dorns The might - y vic-tor's brow.
2. The King of kings, and Lord of lords And heav'n's e - ter - nal Light;
3. To whom he man - i - fests his love And grants his Name to know.

4. To them the cross with all its shame,
With all its grace is giv'n;
Their name, an everlasting name;
Their joy, the joy of heav'n.

ALTERNATE EVENING HYMN

Based on Psalm 1
Nichol Grieve, 1940

C.M.

Dunfermline
Scottish Psalter, 1615

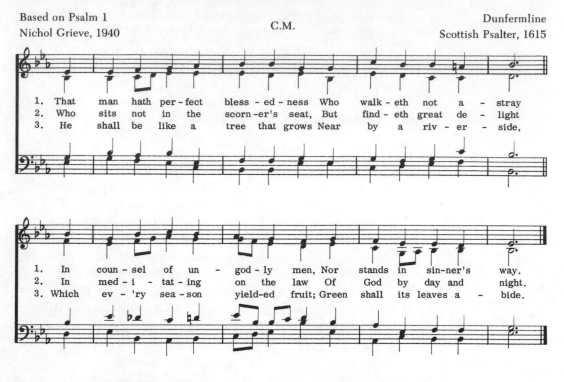

1. That man hath per-fect bless-ed-ness Who walk-eth not a-stray
2. Who sits not in the scorn-er's seat, But find-eth great de-light
3. He shall be like a tree that grows Near by a riv-er-side,

1. In coun-sel of un-god-ly men, Nor stands in sin-ner's way.
2. In med-i-tat-ing on the law Of God by day and night.
3. Which ev-'ry sea-son yield-ed fruit; Green shall its leaves a-bide.

4. He prospereth in all he does;
    The wicked are not so,
    For they are like the empty chaff
    By winds swept to and fro.

5. For evil-doers shall not stand
    When judgment draweth near;
    Nor in assemblies of the just
    Shall godless men appear.

6. The Lord takes knowledge of the way
    In which the righteous go:
    The course which men of sin pursue
    Ends in their overthrow.

Readings

1. Pastors: A reading from the letter of blessed Paul the Apostle to the Colossians (1:24–29): I find my joy in the suffering I endure for you. In my own flesh I fill up what is lacking in the sufferings of Christ for the sake of his body, the church. I became a minister of this church through the commission God gave me to preach among you his word in its fullness, that mystery hidden from ages and generations past but now revealed to his holy ones. God has willed to make known to them the glory beyond price which this mystery brings to the Gentiles—the mystery of

Christ in you, your hope of glory. This is the Christ we proclaim while we admonish all men and teach them in the full measure of wisdom, hoping to make every man complete in Christ. For this work and struggle, impelled by that energy of his which is so powerful a force within me. This is the word of the Lord.

All: Thanks be to God.

2. Saints: A reading from the first letter of blessed Paul the Apostle to the Corinthians (9:24–27): You know that while all the runners in the stadium take part in the race, the award goes to one man. In that case, run so as to win! Athletes deny themselves all sorts of things. They do this to win a crown of leaves that withers, but we a crown that is imperishable. I do not run like a man who loses sight of the finish line. I do not fight as if I were shadowboxing. What I do is discipline my own body and master it, for fear that after having preached to others I myself should be rejected. This is the word of the Lord.

All: Thanks be to God.

Or: A reading from the first letter of blessed Paul the Apostle to the Corinthians (15:50–58): Flesh and blood cannot inherit the kingdom of God. . . . This corruptible body must be clothed with incorruptibility, this mortal body with immortality. When the corruptible frame takes on incorruptibility and the mortal immortality, then will the saying of Scripture be fulfilled: "Death is swallowed up in victory." "O death, where is your victory? O death, where is your sting?" The sting of death is sin, and sin gets its power from the law. But thanks be to God who has given us the victory through our Lord Jesus Christ. Be steadfast and persevering, my beloved brothers, fully engaged in the work of the Lord. You know that your toil is not in vain when it is done in the Lord. This is the word of the Lord.

All: Thanks be to God.

Or: A reading from the letter of blessed Paul the Apostle to the Philippians (3:17–21): Be imitators of me, my brothers. Take as your guide those who follow the example that we set. Unfortunately, many go about in a way which shows them to be enemies of the cross of Christ. I have often said this to you before; this time I say it with tears. Such as these will end in disaster! Their god is their belly and their glory is their shame. I am talking about those who are set upon the things of this world. As you well know, we have our citizenship in heaven; it is from there that we eagerly await the coming of our Savior, the Lord Jesus Christ. He will give a new form to this lowly body of ours and remake it according to the pattern of his glorified body, by his power to subject everything to himself. This is the word of the Lord.

All: Thanks be to God.

Gospel Canticle

CANTICLE OF MARY

1. Pastors

Who ev – er ful-fills and teach-es these com-mands shall be great in the king-dom of God.

2. Saints

He is like a wise man who built his house on rock.

Or:

Blest are they who hear the word of God and keep it.

Intercessions

1. In peace, let us pray to the Lord.

All: Lord, have mercy.

2. Commemorating the saints and in union with them all, let us pray to the Lord.

3. With the great Mother of God, Mary most holy, with John the Forerunner and Stephen the Protomartyr, let us pray to the Lord.

4. With blessed Peter and Paul and the glorious choir of Apostles, let us pray to the Lord.

5. With the white-robed army of martyrs who shed their blood for Christ, let us pray to the Lord.

6. With the holy ascetics who lived for God alone, let us pray to the Lord.

7. With the valiant company of confessors who bore witness to the faith, let us pray to the Lord.

8. With the souls of all the just made perfect, let us pray to the Lord.

9. For all who have fallen asleep in Christ in the true faith, let us pray to the Lord.

10. Help, save, pity and defend us, O God, by your grace. *(Pause)*

11. Rejoicing in the fellowship of the Blessed Virgin Mary, of St. *Name,* and of all the saints, let us commend ourselves, one another, and our whole life to Christ our Lord.

All: To you, O Lord.

Collects

1. Pastors: Good Shepherd, unfailing provider for the flock you have chosen, bless and preserve your church by the merits and prayers of the holy pastors who have so worthily served you; through Jesus Christ our Lord.

All: Amen.

2. Saints: Holy God and Father, as we celebrate the feast of blessed *Name,* help us by his (her) example and intercession to serve you with heartfelt devotion; through Jesus Christ our Lord.

All: Amen.

Or: O God our Savior, make us imitators of the models of holiness you have raised up in your church that we may become perfect followers of your blessed Son, our Lord Jesus Christ, who lives and reigns with you and the Holy Spirit, one God, for ever and ever.

All: Amen.

Blessing

1. May Christ, the King of all saints, bless you and keep/you.

All: Amen.
2. May the Author of all life and holiness graciously smile/upon you.

All: Amen.
3. May the/Lord grant you peace.

All: Amen.

The Office of the Dead—Morning Prayer

Invitatory

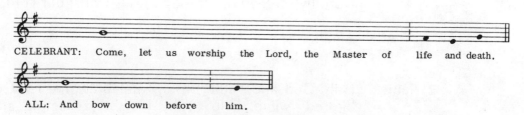

CELEBRANT: Come, let us worship the Lord, the Master of life and death.

ALL: And bow down before him.

MORNING HYMN

James Quinn, S.J., 1969

10 10.10 10.10 10

Unde et Memores
William H. Monk, 1875, alt.

May flights of an-gels lead you on your way To par-a-dise, and heav'n's e-ter-nal day! May mar-tyrs greet you af-ter death's dark night, And bid you en-ter in-to Si-on's light! May choirs of an-gels sing you to your rest With once poor Laz'-rus, now for ev-er blest!

Celebrant: The Lord be with you.

All: And also with you.

The prayer follows immediately.

Merciful Father, the Creator and Redeemer of all the faithful, grant forgiveness of sins to the souls of your departed servants, so that through our loving prayers they may obtain the pardon which they have always desired; through Jesus Christ, your Son, our Lord, who lives and reigns with you and the Holy Spirit, one God, for ever and ever.

All: Amen.

Psalmody

The psalms are taken from Friday Morning Praise, p. 96 ff.

Reading

A reading from the first letter of blessed Paul the Apostle to the Thessalonians (4:13–17): We would have you be clear about those who sleep in death, brothers; otherwise you might yield to grief, like those who have no hope. For if we believe that Jesus died and rose, God will bring forth with him from the dead those also who have fallen asleep believing in him. We say to you, as if the Lord himself had said it, that we who live, who survive until his coming, will in no way have an advantage over those who have fallen asleep. No, the Lord himself will come down from heaven at the word of command, at the sound of the archangel's voice and God's trumpet; and those who have died in Christ will rise first. Then we the living, the survivors, will be caught up with them in the clouds to meet the Lord in the air. Thenceforth we shall be with the Lord unceasingly. Console one another with this message. This is the word of the Lord.

All: Thanks be to God.

Other selections: Wisdom 3:1-9; 4:7-14; Isaiah 25: 6-9; Daniel 12:1-3; II Macc 12:43-46

Gospel Canticle

CANTICLE OF ZECHARIAH

I am the res-ur-rec-tion and the life: who-ev-er be-lieves in me will nev-er die.

Intercessions

1. In peace, let us pray to the Lord.

R: Lord, have mercy.

2. For the mercy of God, the kingdom of heaven, and the remission of all sins and transgressions, let us pray to the Lord.

3. For the resurrection of the body and life everlasting with all the saints, let us pray to the Lord.

4. For a place of refreshment, light and peace where there is no pain, grief or sighing, let us pray to the Lord.

5. For the final destruction of sin, death and the grave, let us pray to the Lord.

6. For our restoration to the paradise for which we yearn, let us pray to the Lord.

7. For grace to walk the narrow way and bear the yoke of the cross, let us pray to the Lord.

8. For the finding of all lost sheep and their safe return to the fold, let us pray to the Lord.

9. For the full restoration of the divine image and the renewal of our original beauty, let us pray to the Lord.

10. For the justification by faith and grace of all the servants of Christ, let us pray to the Lord.

11. For peace for our brother (sister), *Name,* who has eaten of the bread of life and drunk the wine of the kingdom, let us pray to the Lord.

12. Help, save, pity and defend us, O God, by your grace. *(Pause)*

13. Rejoicing in the fellowship of the Blessed Virgin Mary and of all the saints, let us commend ourselves, one another, and our whole life to Christ our Lord.

All: To you, O Lord.

Celebrant: Christ, our true God, Lord of the living and the dead, through the intercession of the great Mother of God, Mary most holy, and of all the saints, establish the soul of your departed servant, *Name,* in the mansions of the just and have mercy on us all, for you are the resurrection and the life and the repose of your departed servants, O Savior of the world, who live and reign with the Father and the Holy Spirit, one God, for ever and ever.

All: Amen.

Blessing

May Christ, our true God, by the grace of his resurrection bless/you and keep you.

R: Amen.

The Office of the Dead—Evensong

EVENING HYMN

Phos Hilaron, Greek 3rd cent.
Tr. William G. Storey

L.M.

Plain Song
Jesu, dulcis memoria

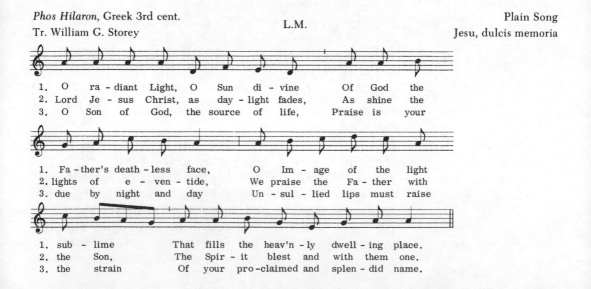

1. O ra-diant Light, O Sun di-vine Of God the
2. Lord Je-sus Christ, as day-light fades, As shine the
3. O Son of God, the source of life, Praise is your

1. Fa-ther's death-less face, O Im-age of the light
2. lights of e-ven-tide, We praise the Fa-ther with
3. due by night and day Un-sul-lied lips must raise

1. sub-lime That fills the heav'n-ly dwell-ing place.
2. the Son, The Spir-it blest and with them one.
3. the strain Of your pro-claimed and splen-did name.

THANKSGIVING

Assistant: The Lord be with you.

All: And also with you.
Blessed are you, O Lord our God, King of the universe, clothed with majesty and glory, wrapped in a robe of light. You made the moon to mark the seasons, the sun to know the hour of its setting. All earth's creatures depend on you for their being and look to you for their sustenance. If you hide your face, they are dismayed; if you take away their breath, they perish and revert to dust, but when you send forth your spirit, they find fresh life again as you continue to sustain the world in wisdom; for you are merciful and you love mankind, and we glorify you, Father, Son and Holy Spirit, now and for ever.

All: Amen.

Psalmody

The psalms are taken from Friday Evensong, p. 104ff.

Reading

A reading from the second letter of blessed Paul the Apostle to the Corinthians (4:16–5:10): We do not lose heart, because our inner being is renewed each day even though our body is being destroyed at the same time. The present burden of our trial is light enough, and earns for us an eternal weight of glory beyond all comparison. We do not fix our gaze on what is seen but on what is unseen. What is seen is transitory; what is unseen lasts forever. Indeed, we know that when the earthly tent in which we dwell is destroyed we have a dwelling provided for us by God, a dwelling in the heavens, not made by hands but to last forever. We groan while we are here, even as we yearn to have our heavenly habitation envelop us. This it will, provided we are found clothed and not naked. While we live in our present tent we groan; we are weighed down because we do not wish to be stripped naked but rather to have the heavenly dwelling envelop us, so that what is mortal may be absorbed by life. God has fashioned us for this very thing and has given us the spirit as a pledge of it. This is the word of the Lord.

All: Thanks be to God.

Other selections: Acts 10:34-43; Romans 5:5-11; 5:17-21; 14:7-9, 10-12; I Cor 15:20-28; 51-57; II Tim 2:8-13; Rev 20:11-21:1; 21:1-7

Gospel Canticle

CANTICLE OF MARY

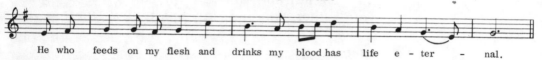

He who feeds on my flesh and drinks my blood has life e - ter - nal.

Intercessions

1. In peace, let us pray to the Lord.

All: Lord, have mercy.

2. For the souls of those who have fallen asleep in Christ in the true faith, let us pray to the Lord.

3. For the precious power of the holy cross to save their souls, let us pray to the Lord.

4. For the remission of all their sins and transgressions, let us pray to the Lord,

5. For full release from all sin and punishment, let us pray to the Lord.

6. For an angel of peace to lead them safely home to paradise, let us pray to the Lord.

7. For the resurrection of the body and life everlasting with all the saints, let us pray to the Lord.

8. For the repose of the soul of our brother (sister), *Name,* let us pray to the Lord.

9. For the final destruction of sin, death and the grave by the power of the risen Christ, let us pray to the Lord.

10. Help, save, pity and defend us, O God, by your grace. *(Pause)*

11. Rejoicing in the fellowship of the Blessed Virgin Mary and of all the faithful departed, let us commend ourselves, one another, and our whole life to Christ our Lord.

All: To you, O Lord.

Celebrant: In your kindness and compassion, O Father of mercies, grant to the souls of those who believed and trusted in you a place of everlasting refreshment, light and peace; through Jesus Christ our Lord.

All: Amen.

Or: May the holy Mother of God and all the saints be our intercessors before the Father in heaven, that he may be pleased to have mercy and compassion upon us his creatures and to conduct us in safety to our heavenly home; through Jesus Christ our Lord.

All: Amen.

Or: Make us worthy, O God of compassion, with all those who have fallen asleep in Christ in the true faith, to bless, praise and thank you, Father, Son and Holy Spirit, now and always and for ever and ever.

All: Amen.

Blessing

1. May Jesus Christ, the Son of the living God, bless you and keep/you.

All: Amen.
2. May the living Bread come down from heaven graciously smile/upon you.

All: Amen.
3. May the/Lord grant you peace.

All: Amen.

Appendix of Additional Psalms

The following psalms provide alternate settings for some of the psalms of the weekly psalter, as well as others not included there. They may be used whenever it is deemed appropriate.

PSALM 4—Night prayer of thanksgiving and joyful confidence in God

Text: The Grail

David F. Wright, O.P.

ANTIPHON: I will lie down in peace, and sleep comes at once.

1. When I call, answer me, O / God, of jus - tice;
   from anguish your released me, have mer / cy and hear me.

   O men, how long will your / hearts be closed,
   will you love what is futile and seek / what is false.

2. It is the Lord who grants favors to those / whom he loves.
   the Lord hears me whenev / er I call him.
   Fear him; do not sin; ponder on your bed / and be still;
   Make justice your sacrifice and trust / in the Lord.

3. "What can bring us happiness?" / man - y say.
   Lift up the light of your face on / us O Lord.
   You have put into my heart a / great - er joy,
   than they have from abundance of wheat / and new wine.

4. I will lie down in peace and sleep / comes at once,
   for you alone, Lord, make me / dwell in safe - ty.
   To the Father, the Son and / Ho - ly Spir - it
   give praise forev / er. A - men.

Celebrant: Let us pray.

Pause for silent prayer.

O God, our Protector, look on the face of your Christ who delivered himself up to redeem mankind. Enable all men everywhere to glorify your name from sunrise to sunset and to offer you an unblemished sacrifice of praise; through the same Jesus Christ our Lord.

All: Amen.

PSALM 8—The grandeur of God and the dignity of the Son of Man

Text: The Grail   Frank Quinn, O.P.

ANTIPHON: How great is your name, O Lord, our God, through all the earth.

1.	Your	MAjesty is	PRAISED above the	HEAVens;	on the
2.	When I see the	HEAVens, the	WORK of your	HANDS,	the
3.	Yet you have	MADE him little	LESS than a	GOD;	with
4.		ALL of them	SHEEP and	CATtle,	yes,
5.	Give	PRAISE to the	FAther al -	MIGHTy,	to his

1. LIPS of	CHILdren and of	BABES	you have found	PRAISE to	
2. MOON and the	STARS which you ar -	RANGED,	what is	MAN that you should	
3. GLOry and	HONor you	CROWNED him,	gave him	POWer over the	
4. EVen the	SAVage	BEASTS,		BIRDS of the	
5. SON, Jesus	CHRIST the	LORD,	to the	SPIRit who	

1. FOIL your	ENemy,	to	SIlence the	FOE and the	REbel.
2. KEEP him in	MIND,	mortal	MAN that you	CARE for	HIM?
3. WORKS of your	HAND,	put	ALL things	UNder his	FEET.
4. AIR and	FISH	that	MAKE their	WAY through the	WAters.
5. DWELLS in our	HEARTS,	both	NOW and for	EVer. A -	MEN.

Celebrant: Let us pray.

Pause for silent prayer.

O God, whose name is blessed from sunrise to sunset, fill our hearts with knowledge of you and make us worthy to sing your praise and thank you for your great glory, that you may be honored and glorified from east to west and from pole to pole for all the ages of ages; through Jesus Christ our Lord.

All: Amen.

PSALM 23

"The Lamb on the throne will shepherd them." (Rev 7:17)

Text: The Grail   Frank Quinn, O.P.

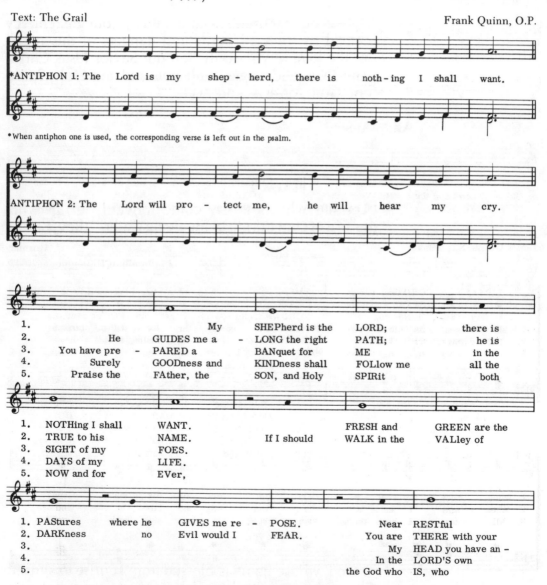

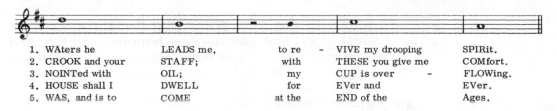

1. WAters he	LEADS me,	to re -	VIVE my drooping	SPIRit.
2. CROOK and your	STAFF;	with	THESE you give me	COMfort.
3. NOINTed with	OIL;	my	CUP is over -	FLOWing.
4. HOUSE shall I	DWELL	for	EVer and	EVer.
5. WAS, and is to	COME	at the	END of the	Ages.

Celebrant: Let us pray.

Pause for silent prayer.

Lighten our darkness, O Lord, and by your great mercy defend us from all perils and dangers of this night, for the love of your only Son our Savior Jesus Christ, who lives and reigns with you and the Holy Spirit, one God, for ever and ever.

All: Amen.

PSALM 42

"Let him who is thirsty come forward; let all who desire it accept the gift of lifegiving water." (Rev 22:17)

James Quinn, S.J., 1969

66.66

Hosmer
Psalteriolum Harmonicum, 1642

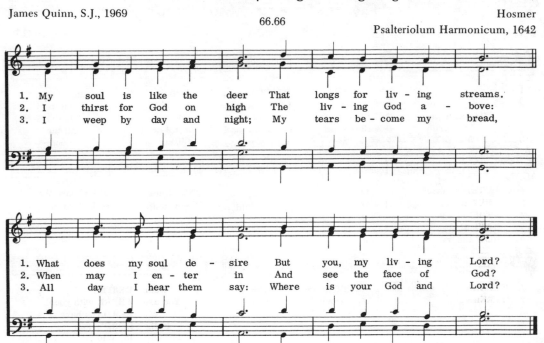

1. My	soul	is	like	the	deer	That	longs	for	liv - ing	streams.
2. I	thirst	for	God	on	high	The	liv - ing	God	a -	bove:
3. I	weep	by	day	and	night;	My	tears	be - come	my	bread,

1. What	does	my soul	de -	sire	But	you,	my	liv - ing	Lord?
2. When	may	I en - ter	in	And	see	the	face	of	God?
3. All	day	I hear them	say:	Where	is	your	God and	Lord?

4. I think of days gone by
    As I pour out my soul:
    God's people I would lead
    Into the house of God.

5. Around me they would sing
    In joy and thankfulness;
    Boundless would be their joy
    Within God's holy house.

6. My soul why are you sad?
    Why do you moan and sigh?
    In him still hope; still praise
    Your Savior and your God.

Celebrant: Let us pray.

Pause for silent prayer.

O God, our rock and our Savior, teach us to put our trust in your loving kindness and in time of trouble to live by hope; through Christ our Lord.

All: Amen.

PSALM 59

"You will suffer in the world. But take courage! I have overcome the world." (Jn 16:33)

Text: The Grail   David F. Wright, O.P.

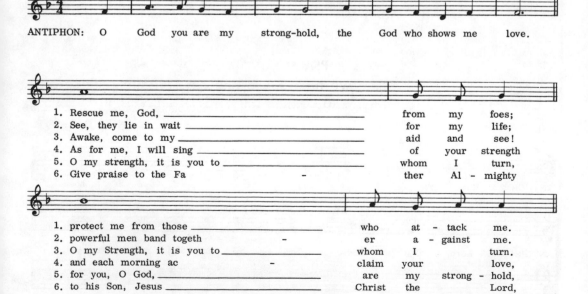

ANTIPHON: O God you are my strong-hold, the God who shows me love.

1. Rescue me, God, _____ from my foes;
2. See, they lie in wait _____ for my life;
3. Awake, come to my _____ aid and see!
4. As for me, I will sing _____ of your strength
5. O my strength, it is you to _____ whom I turn,
6. Give praise to the Fa - ther Al - mighty

1. protect me from those _____ who at - tack me.
2. powerful men band togeth - er a - gainst me.
3. O my Strength, it is you to _____ whom I turn.
4. and each morning ac - claim your love,
5. for you, O God, _____ are my strong - hold,
6. to his Son, Jesus _____ Christ the Lord,

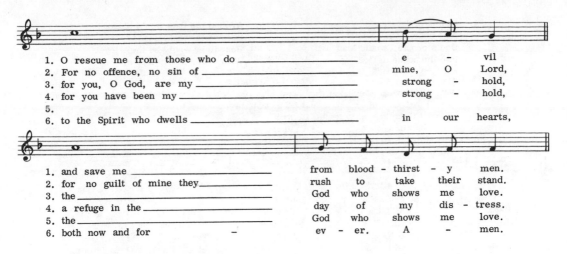

1. O rescue me from those who do ____ e - vil
2. For no offence, no sin of ____ mine, O Lord,
3. for you, O God, are my ____ strong - hold,
4. for you have been my ____ strong - hold,
5.
6. to the Spirit who dwells ____ in our hearts,

1. and save me ____ from blood - thirst - y men.
2. for no guilt of mine they ____ rush to take their stand.
3. the ____ God who shows me love.
4. a refuge in the ____ day of my dis - tress.
5. the ____ God who shows me love.
6. both now and for   – ev - er. A - men.

Celebrant: Let us pray.

Pause for silent prayer.

Almighty and everlasting God, who appointed your only-begotten Son the Savior of the world, and willed to accept the free gift of his blood for our redemption, grant that we may so venerate this price of our salvation that we may be defended on earth by its power from the evils of this present life and be made glad in heaven by its everlasting fruit; through the same Christ our Lord.

All: Amen.

PSALM 84

"Here we have no lasting city; we are seeking one which is to come." (Heb 13:14)

Text: The Grail   Frank Quinn, O.P.

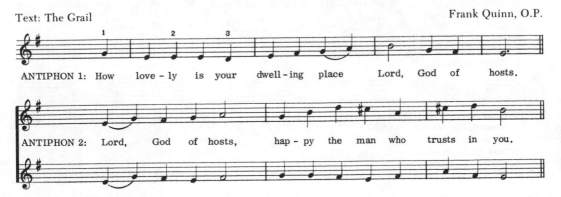

ANTIPHON 1: How love - ly is your dwell - ing place Lord, God of hosts.

ANTIPHON 2: Lord, God of hosts, hap - py the man who trusts in you.

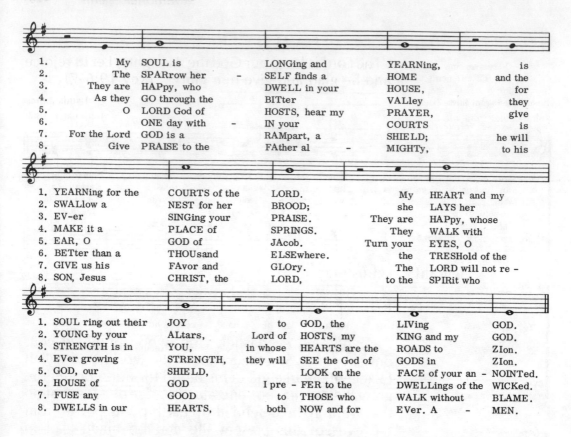

1. My SOUL is LONGing and YEARNing, is YEARNing for the COURTS of the LORD. My HEART and my SOUL ring out their JOY to GOD, the LIVing GOD.
2. The SPARrow her - SELF finds a HOME and the SWALlow a NEST for her BROOD; she LAYS her YOUNG by your ALtars, Lord of HOSTS, my KING and my GOD.
3. They are HAPpy, who DWELL in your HOUSE, for EV-er SINGing your PRAISE. They are HAPpy, whose STRENGTH is in YOU, in whose HEARTS are the ROADS to ZIon.
4. As they GO through the BITter VALley they MAKE it a PLACE of SPRINGS. They WALK with EVer growing STRENGTH, they will SEE the God of GODS in ZIon.
5. O LORD God of HOSTS, hear my PRAYER, give EAR, O GOD of JAcob. Turn your EYES, O GOD, our SHIELD, LOOK on the FACE of your an - NOINTed.
6. ONE day with - IN your COURTS is BETter than a THOUsand ELSEwhere. the TRESHold of the HOUSE of GOD I pre - FER to the DWELLings of the WICKed.
7. For the Lord GOD is a RAMpart, a SHIELD; he will GIVE us his FAvor and GLOry. The LORD will not re - FUSE any GOOD to THOSE who WALK without BLAME.
8. Give PRAISE to the FAther al - MIGHTy, to his SON, Jesus CHRIST, the LORD, to the SPIRit who DWELLS in our HEARTS, both NOW and for EVer. A - MEN.

Celebrant: Let us pray.

Distinct pause for silent prayer.

O God, support us all the day long of this troubled life, until the shadows lengthen and the evening comes, the busy world is hushed, the fever of life is over and our work is done. Then, Lord, in your mercy, grant us a safe lodging, a holy rest, and peace at the last; through Jesus Christ our Lord.

All: Amen.

PSALM 93

"The Lord is king, our God the Almighty, Let us rejoice and be glad and give him glory." (Rev 19:6–7)

Based on Psalm 93
John Keble, 1839, alt.

87.87.87

Lauda anima
John Goss, 1869

1. God, the Lord, is King for ev - er, Robed in
2. In her ev - er - last - ing sta - tion Earth is
3. With all tones of wa - ters blend - ing Glo - rious

1. his own glo - rious light; He has robed him - self with
2. poised, to swerve no more; You have laid your throne's foun -
3. is the break - ing deep; Glo - rious, beau - teous, with - out

1. pow - er, And has gird - ed him with might. Al - le - lu - ia!
2. da - tion From all time where thought can soar. Al - le - lu - ia!
3. end - ing God, who reigns on heav'n's high steep. Al - le - lu - ia!

1. Al - le - lu - ia! God is King in depth and height!
2. Al - le - lu - ia! Lord, you are for - ev - er - more!
3. Al - le - lu - ia! Songs of o - cean nev - er sleep.

4. Lord, the words your lips are telling
    Are the perfect verity;
    Of your high eternal dwelling,
    Holiness shall inmate be:
    Alleluia! Alleluia!
    Pure is all that lives with thee.

Celebrant: Let us pray.

Pause for silent prayer.

Lord God, King of the universe, robed in majesty, girded with power, make us trust in your decrees and clothe us in the holiness that befits your house; through Christ our Lord.

All: Amen.

PSALM 130

"Christ came into the world to save sinners." (1 Tim 1:15)

Text: The Grail

Frank Quinn, O.P.

will re-deem from all its in-iq-ui-ty.

5. Praise the Fa-ther, the Son, and Ho-ly Spir-it both

now and for-ev-er, the God who is,___ who was, and

is to come at the end of the a-ges.

Celebrant: Let us pray.

Pause for Silent prayer.

Grant, O Father, that as we are baptized into the death of your beloved Son, our Savior Jesus Christ, so by continually dying to our corrupt affections, we may be buried with him; and that, through the grave and gate of death, we may pass to our joyful resurrection; for his merits, who died and was buried and rose again for us, the same Jesus Christ our Lord.

All: Amen.

PSALM 134

"Jesus spent the night in communion with God." (Lk 6:12)

Text: The Grail   Frank Quinn, O.P.

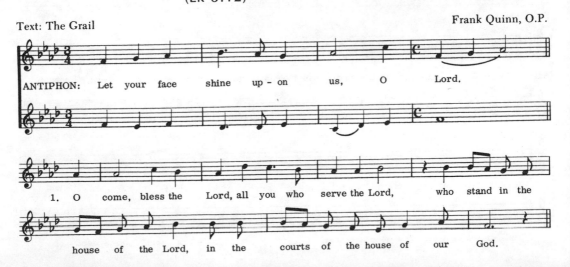

ANTIPHON: Let your face shine up-on us, O Lord.

1. O come, bless the Lord, all you who serve the Lord, who stand in the

house of the Lord, in the courts of the house of our God.

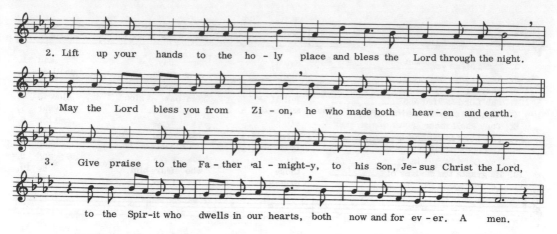

2. Lift up your hands to the ho-ly place and bless the Lord through the night.

May the Lord bless you from Zi-on, he who made both heav-en and earth.

3. Give praise to the Fa-ther al-might-y, to his Son, Je-sus Christ the Lord,

to the Spir-it who dwells in our hearts, both now and for ev-er. A men.

Celebrant: Let us pray.

Pause for silent prayer.

O God, whose name is blessed from sunrise to sunset, fill our hearts with knowledge of you and make us worthy to sing your praise and thank you for your great glory, that you may be enthroned upon the praises of your people and honored and glorified for all the ages of ages; through Jesus Christ our Lord.

All: Amen.

PSALM 145

"God raised us up . . . that in the ages to come he might display the great wealth of his favor, manifested by his kindness to us in Christ Jesus." (Eph 2:7)

Text: The Grail

Frank Quinn, O.P.

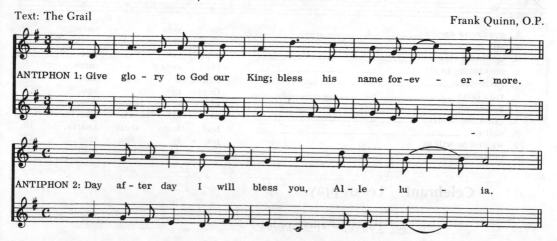

ANTIPHON 1: Give glo-ry to God our King; bless his name for-ev - er - more.

ANTIPHON 2: Day af-ter day I will bless you, Al-le - lu - ia.

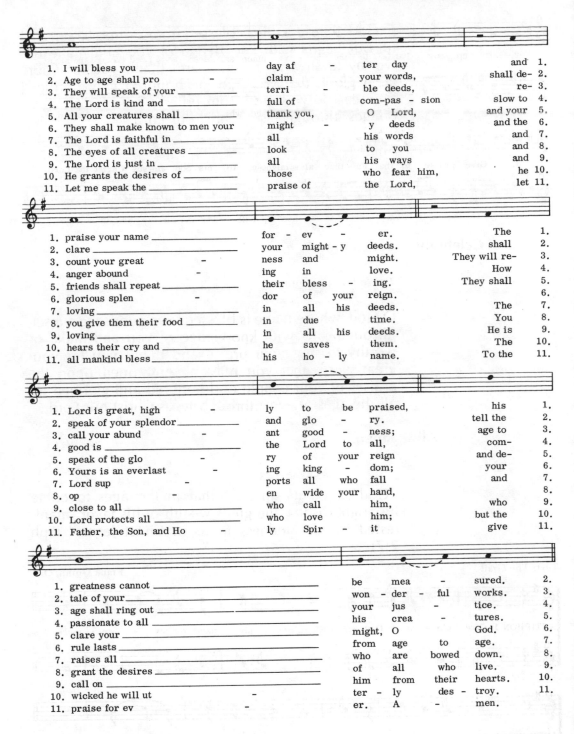

1. I will bless you _____ day af – ter day and 1.
2. Age to age shall pro – claim your words, shall de- 2.
3. They will speak of your _____ terri – ble deeds, re- 3.
4. The Lord is kind and _____ full of com-pas - sion slow to 4.
5. All your creatures shall _____ thank you, O Lord, and your 5.
6. They shall make known to men your might – y deeds and the 6.
7. The Lord is faithful in _____ all his words and 7.
8. The eyes of all creatures _____ look to you and 8.
9. The Lord is just in _____ all his ways and 9.
10. He grants the desires of _____ those who fear him, he 10.
11. Let me speak the _____ praise of the Lord, let 11.

1. praise your name _____ for - ev – er. The 1.
2. clare _____ your might - y deeds. shall 2.
3. count your great – ness and might. They will re- 3.
4. anger abound – ing in love. How 4.
5. friends shall repeat _____ their bless – ing. They shall 5.
6. glorious splen – dor of your reign. 6.
7. loving _____ in all his deeds. The 7.
8. you give them their food _____ in due time. You 8.
9. loving _____ in all his deeds. He is 9.
10. hears their cry and _____ he saves them. The 10.
11. all mankind bless _____ his ho - ly name. To the 11.

1. Lord is great, high – ly to be praised, his 1.
2. speak of your splendor _____ and glo - ry. tell the 2.
3. call your abund – ant good - ness; age to 3.
4. good is _____ the Lord to all, com- 4.
5. speak of the glo – ry of your reign and de- 5.
6. Yours is an everlast – ing king - dom; your 6.
7. Lord sup – ports all who fall and 7.
8. op – en wide your hand, 8.
9. close to all _____ who call him, who 9.
10. Lord protects all _____ who love him; but the 10.
11. Father, the Son, and Ho – ly Spir - it give 11.

1. greatness cannot _____ be mea – sured. 2.
2. tale of your _____ won - der - ful works. 3.
3. age shall ring out _____ your jus – tice. 4.
4. passionate to all _____ his crea – tures. 5.
5. clare your _____ might, O God. 6.
6. rule lasts _____ from age to age. 7.
7. raises all _____ who are bowed down. 8.
8. grant the desires _____ of all who live. 9.
9. call on _____ him from their hearts. 10.
10. wicked he will ut – ter - ly des - troy. 11.
11. praise for ev – er. A - men.

Celebrant: Let us pray.

Pause for silent prayer.

O God, whose name is blessed from sunrise to sunset, fill our hearts with knowledge of you and make us worthy to sing your praise and thank you for your great glory, that you may be honored and glorified from east to west and from pole to pole for all ages of ages; through Jesus Christ our Lord.

All: Amen.

Table of Scripture Readings

Following ancient tradition, sacred scripture is read publicly in the liturgy not only in the celebration of the Eucharist but also in the Divine Office. This liturgical reading of scripture is of the greatest importance for all Christians because it is offered by the Church herself and not by the decision or whim of a single individual. "Within the cycle of a year" the mystery of Christ is unfolded by his Bride. . . . In liturgical celebrations prayer always accompanies the reading of sacred scripture. In this way the reading may bear greater fruit, and conversely prayer, especially through the psalms, may be more fully developed by the reading and encourage more intense devotion.

The General Instruction on the Liturgy of the Hours,
140

Table of Scripture Readings
ADVENT

		Year 1	Year 2
		ADVENT SEASON TO 16 DECEMBER	
Week I	Sunday	Is 6:1–13	Is 1:1–18
	Monday	Is 7:1–17	Is 1:21–2:5
	Tuesday	Is 8:1–18	Is 2:6–22; 4:2–6
	Wednesday	Is 9:1b–7	Is 5:1–7
	Thursday	Is 10:5–21	Is 16:1–5; 17:4–8
	Friday	Is 11:10–16	Is 19:16–25
	Saturday	Is 13:1–22a	Is 21:6–12
Week II	Sunday	Is 14:1–21	Is 22:8b–23
	Monday	Is 34:1–17	Is 24:1–18a
	Tuesday	Is 35:1–10	Is 24:18b–25:5
	Wednesday	Ruth 1:1–22	Is 25:6–26:6
	Thursday	Ruth 2:1–13	Is 26:7–21
	Friday	Ruth 2:14–23	Is 27:1–13
	Saturday	Ruth 3:1–18	Is 29:1–8
Week III	Sunday	Ruth 4:1–22	Is 29:13–24
	Monday	1 Chr 17:1–15	Is 30:18–26
	Tuesday	Mic 4:1–7	Is 30:27–31:9
	Wednesday	Mic 5:1–8	Is 32:1–8
	Thursday	Mic 7:7–13	Is 32:9–33:6
	Friday	Mic 7:14–20	Is 33:7–24

.FROM 17–24 DECEMBER

Dec. 17	Is 40:1–11	Is 45:1–13
Dec. 18	Is 40:12–18, 21–31	Is 46:1–13
Dec. 19	Is 41:8–20	Is 47:1–15
Dec. 20	Is 41:21–29	Is 48:1–11
Dec. 21	Is 42:10–25	Is 48:12–21; 49:9b–13
Dec. 22	Is 43:1–13	Is 49:14–50:1
Dec. 23	Is 43:19–28	Is 51:1–11
Dec. 24	Is 44:1–8, 21–23	Is 51:17–52:10

CHRISTMASTIDE

Dec. 25 The Nativity of our Lord Is 11:1–10
Sunday within the Octave of Christmas: Feast of the Holy Family Eph 5:21–6:4
Dec. 26 Stephen the Protomartyr Acts 6:8–7:2, 44–59
Dec. 27 John, Apostle and Evang. I Jn. 1:1–2:3
Dec. 28 The Holy Innocents Exodus 1:8–16, 22

	Year 1	**Year 2**
Dec. 29	Col 1:1–14	S of S 1:1–8
Dec. 30	Col 1:15–2:3	S of S 1:9–2:7
Dec. 31	Col 2:4–15	S of S 2:8–3:5
Jan. 1	Solemnity of Mary Mother of God Heb 2:9–17	
Jan. 2	Col 2:16–3:4	S of S 4:1–5:1

In places where the Epiphany is celebrated on the Sunday occurring between 2–8 January, the readings given for 7–12 January are read after the Epiphany, the following being omitted:

Jan. 3	Col 3:5–16	S of S 5:2–6:2
Jan. 4	Col 3:17–4:1	S of S 6:3–7:10
Jan. 5	Col 4:2–18	S of S 7:11–8:7

Jan. 6 (*in places where the Epiphany is celebrated on Jan. 7 or 8*)

	Is 42:1–8	Is 49:1–9

Jan. 7 (*in places where the Epiphany is celebrated on Jan. 7 or 8*)

	Is 61:1–11	Is 54:1–17
Jan. 6	The Epiphany of our Lord Is 60:1–22	

The readings assigned to 7–12 January are read on the days which follow the solemnity of the Epiphany, even when this is kept on the Sunday, until the following Saturday. From the Monday after the Sunday on which the Baptism of our Lord is celebrated, i.e. the Sunday occurring after 6 January, the readings of the weeks of the year are begun, omitting any which remain of those assigned to the ferias between 7–12 January.

	Year 1	**Year 2**
Jan. 7 *or Mon.* *after* Epiphany	Is 61:1–11	Is 54:1–17
Jan. 8 *or Tues.* *after* Epiphany	Is 62:1–12	Is 55:1–13
Jan. 9 *or Wed.* *after* Epiphany	Is 63:7–64:1	Is 56:1–8
Jan. 10 *or Thurs.* *after* Epiphany	Is 64:1–12	Is 59:15–21
Jan. 11 *or Fri.* *after* Epiphany	Is 65:13–25	Baruch 4:5–29

		Year 1	Year 2

Jan. 12 *or Sat.*
after
Epiphany   Is 66:5–14a, 18–23 Baruch 4:30–5:9
Sunday occurring after Jan. 6: Feast of the Baptism of our Lord
Is 42:1–8; 49:1–9

LENT

Ash Wednesday Is 58:1–14

		Year 1	Year 2
	Thursday	Deut 1:1, 6–18	Exod 1:1–22
	Friday	Deut 4:1–8, 32–40	Exod 2:1–22
	Saturday	Deut 5:1–22	Exod 3:1–20
Week I	Sunday	Deut 6:4–25	Exod 5:1–6:1
	Monday	Deut 7:6–14; 8:1–6	Exod 6:2–13
	Tuesday	Deut 9:7–21, 25–29	Exod 6:29–7:24
	Wednesday	Deut 10:12–11:7, 26–28	Exod 10:21–11:10
	Thursday	Deut 12:1–14	Exod 12:1–20
	Friday	Deut 15:1–18	Exod 12:21–36
	Saturday	Deut 16:1–17	Exod 12:37–49; 13:11–16
Week II	Sunday	Deut 18:1–22	Exod 13:17–14:9
	Monday	Deut 24:1–25:4	Exod 14:10–31
	Tuesday	Deut 26:1–19	Exod 16:1–18, 35
	Wednesday	Deut 29:2–6, 10–29	Exod 17:1–16
	Thursday	Deut 30:1–20	Exod 18:13–27
	Friday	Deut 31:1–15, 23	Exod 19:1–19; 20:18–21
	Saturday	Deut 32:48–52; 34:1–12	Exod 20:1–17
Week III	Sunday	Heb 1:1–2:4	Exod 22:20–23:9
	Monday	Heb 2:5–18	Exod 24:1–18
	Tuesday	Heb 3:1–19	Exod 32:1–5, 15–34
	Wednesday	Heb 4:1–13	Exod 33:7–11, 18–23; 34:5–9, 29–35
	Thursday	Heb 4:14–5:10	Exod 34:10–28
	Friday	Heb 5:11–6:8	Exod 35:30–36:1; 37:1–9
	Saturday	Heb 6:9–20	Exod 40:16–38
Week IV	Sunday	Heb 7:1–11	Lev 8:1–17; 9:22–24
	Monday	Heb 7:11–28	Lev 16:2–27
	Tuesday	Heb 8:1–13	Lev 19:1–18, 31–37

		Year 1	**Year 2**
	Wednesday	Heb 9:1–14	Lev 26:3–17, 38–46
	Thursday	Heb 9:15–28	Num 3:1–13; 8:5–11
	Friday	Heb 10:1–10	Num 9:15–10:10, 33–36
	Saturday	Heb 10:11–25	Num 11:4–6, 10–33
Week V	Sunday	Heb 10:26–39	Num 12:1–15
	Monday	Heb 11:1–19	Num 12:16–13:3, 17–33
	Tuesday	Heb 11:20–31	Num 14:1–25
	Wednesday	Heb 11:32–40	Num 16:1–35
	Thursday	Heb 12:1–13	Num 20:1–13; 21:4–9
	Friday	Heb 12:14–29	Num 22:1–8a, 20–35
	Saturday	Heb 13:1–25	Num 24:1–19
Holy Week	Sunday	Is 50:4–51:3	Jer 22:1–8; 23:1–8
	Monday	Is 52:13–53:12	Jer 26:1–15
	Tuesday	Lam 1:1–12, 18–20	Jer 8:13–9:9
	Wednesday	Lam 2:1–10	Jer 11:18–12:13
	Thursday	Lam 2:11–22	Jer 15:10–21
	Friday	Lam 3:1–33	Jer 16:1–15
	Saturday	Lam 5:1–22	Jer 20:7–18

EASTERTIDE

Easter Sunday: Any one of the Vigil readings may be used

		Year 1	**Year 2**
Easter Week	Monday	1 Pet 1:1–21	Acts 1:1–26
	Tuesday	1 Pet 1:22–2:10	Acts 2:1–21
	Wednesday	1 Pet 2:11–25	Acts 2:22–41
	Thursday	1 Pet 3:1–17	Acts 2:42–3:11
	Friday	1 Pet 3:18–4:11	Acts 3:12–4:4
	Saturday	1 Pet 4:12–5:14	Acts 4:5–31

		Year 1	**Year 2**
Week II	Sunday	Col 3:1–17	Col 3:1–17
	Monday	Rev 1:1–20	Acts 4:32–5:16
	Tuesday	Rev 2:1–11	Acts 5:17–42
	Wednesday	Rev 2:12–29	Acts 6:1–15
	Thursday	Rev 3:1–22	Acts 7:1–16
	Friday	Rev 4:1–11	Acts 7:17–43
	Saturday	Rev 5:1–14	Acts 7:44–8:3
Week III	Sunday	Rev 6:1–17	Acts 8:4–25
	Monday	Rev 7:1–17	Acts 8:26–40
	Tuesday	Rev 8:1–13	Acts 9:1–22
	Wednesday	Rev 9:1–12	Acts 9:23–43

		Year 1	Year 2
	Thursday	Rev 9:13–21	Acts 10:1–33
	Friday	Rev 10:1–11	Acts 10:34–11:4, 18
	Saturday	Rev 11:1–19	Acts 11:19–30
Week IV	Sunday	Rev 12:1–17	Acts 12:1–23
	Monday	Rev 13:1–18	Acts 12:24–13:14a
	Tuesday	Rev 14:1–13	Acts 13:14b–43
	Wednesday	Rev 14:14–15:4	Acts 13:44–14:7
	Thursday	Rev 15:5–16:21	Acts 14:8–15:4
	Friday	Rev 17:1–18	Acts 15:5–35
	Saturday	Rev 18:1–20	Acts 15:36–16:15
Week V	Sunday	Rev 18:21–19:10	Acts 16:16–40
	Monday	Rev 19:11–21	Acts 17:1–18
	Tuesday	Rev 20:1–15	Acts 17:19–34
	Wednesday	Rev 21:1–8	Acts 18:1–28
	Thursday	Rev 21:9–27	Acts 19:1–20
	Friday	Rev 22:1–9	Acts 19:21–41
	Saturday	Rev 22:10–21	Acts 20:1–16
Week VI	Sunday	1 Jn 1:1–10	Acts 20:17–38
	Monday	1 Jn 2:1–11	Acts 21:1–26
	Tuesday	1 Jn 2:12–17	Acts 21:27–39
	Wednesday	1 Jn 2:18–29	Acts 21:40–22:21
	Thursday	The ascension of Our Lord	Eph 4:1–24
	Friday	1 Jn 3:1–10	Acts 22:22–23:11
	Saturday	1 Jn 3:11–17	Acts 23:12–35
Week VII	Sunday	1 Jn 3:18–24	Acts 24:1–27
	Monday	1 Jn 4:1–10	Acts 25:1–27
	Tuesday	1 Jn 4:11–21	Acts 26:1–32
	Wednesday	1 Jn 5:1–12	Acts 27:1–20
	Thursday	1 Jn 5:13–21	Acts 27:21–44
	Friday	2 Jn	Acts 28:1–14
	Saturday	3 Jn	Acts 28:15–31
	Penetcost Sunday Rom 8:5–27		

TIME THROUGHOUT THE YEAR

Week I	Monday	Rom 1:1–17	Gen 1:1–2:4a
	Tuesday	Rom 1:18–32	Gen 2:4b–25
	Wednesday	Rom 2:1–16	Gen 3:1–24
	Thursday	Rom 2:17–29	Gen 4:1–24
	Friday	Rom 3:1–20	Gen 6:5–22; 7:17–24
	Saturday	Rom 3:21–31	Gen 8:1–22

		Year 1	Year 2
Week II	Sunday	Rom 4:1–25	Gen 9:1–17
	Monday	Rom 5:1–11	Gen 11:1–26
	Tuesday	Rom 5:12–21	Gen 12:1–9; 13:2–18
	Wednesday	Rom 6:1–11	Gen 14:1–24
	Thursday	Rom 6:12–23	Gen 15:1–21
	Friday	Rom 7:1–13	Gen 16:1–16
	Saturday	Rom 7:14–25	Gen 17:1–27
Week III	Sunday	Rom 8:1–17	Gen 18:1–33
	Monday	Rom 8:18–39	Gen 19:1–17, 23–29
	Tuesday	Rom 9:1–18	Gen 21:1–21
	Wednesday	Rom 9:19–33	Gen 22:1–19
	Thursday	Rom 10:1–21	Gen 24:1–27
	Friday	Rom 11:1–12	Gen 24:33–41, 49–67
	Saturday	Rom 11:13–24	Gen 25:7–11, 19–34
Week IV	Sunday	Rom 11:25–36	Gen 27:1–29
	Monday	Rom 12:1–21	Gen 27:30–45
	Tuesday	Rom 13:1–14	Gen 28:10–29:14
	Wednesday	Rom 14:1–23	Gen 31:1–21
	Thursday	Rom 15:1–13	Gen 32:3–30
	Friday	Rom 15:14–33	Gen 35:1–29
	Saturday	Rom 16:1–27	Gen 37:2–4, 12–36
Week V	Sunday	1 Cor 1:1–17	Gen 39:1–23
	Monday	1 Cor 1:18–31	Gen 41:1–15, 25–43
	Tuesday	1 Cor 2:1–16	Gen 41:55–42:26
	Wednesday	1 Cor 3:1–23	Gen 43:1–17, 26–34
	Thursday	1 Cor 4:1–21	Gen 44:1–20, 30–34
	Friday	1 Cor 5:1–13	Gen 45:1–15, 21b–28; 46:1–7
	Saturday	1 Cor 6:1–11	Gen 49:1–28, 33
Week VI	Sunday	1 Cor 6:12–29	1 Thess 1:1–2:12
	Monday	1 Cor 7:1–24	1 Thess 2:13–3:13
	Tuesday	1 Cor 7:25–40	1 Thess 4:1–18
	Wednesday	1 Cor 8:1–13	1 Thess 5:1–28
	Thursday	1 Cor 9:1–18	2 Thess 1:1–12
	Friday	1 Cor 9:19–27	2 Thess 2:1–17
	Saturday	1 Cor 10:1–14	2 Thess 3:1–18
Week VII	Sunday	1 Cor 10:14–11:1	2 Cor 1:1–14
	Monday	1 Cor 11:2–16	2 Cor 1:15–2:11
	Tuesday	1 Cor 11:17–34	2 Cor 2:12–3:6
	Wednesday	1 Cor 12:1–11	2 Cor 3:7–4:4
	Thursday	1 Cor 12:12–31	2 Cor 4:5–18

		Year 1	Year 2
	Friday	1 Cor 12:31–13:13	2 Cor 5:1–21
	Saturday	1 Cor 14:1–19	2 Cor 6:1–7:1
Week VIII	Sunday	1 Cor 14:20–40	2 Cor 7:2–16
	Monday	1 Cor 15:1–19	2 Cor 8:1–24
	Tuesday	1 Cor 15:20–34	2 Cor 9:1–15
	Wednesday	1 Cor 15:35–58	2 Cor 10:1–11:6
	Thursday	1 Cor 16:1–24	2 Cor 11:7–29
	Friday	Jas 1:1–18	2 Cor 11:30–12:13
	Saturday	Jas 1:19–27	2 Cor 12:14–13:14
Week IX	Sunday	Jas 2:1–13	Gal 1:1–12
	Monday	Jas 2:14–26	Gal 1:13–2:10
	Tuesday	Jas 3:1–12	Gal 2:11–3:14
	Wednesday	Jas 3:13–18	Gal 3:15–4:7
	Thursday	Jas 4:1–12	Gal 4:8–5:1a
	Friday	Jas 4:13–5:11	Gal 5:1b–25
	Saturday	Jas 5:12–20	Gal 5:25–6:18
Week X	Sunday	Sir 46:1–10	Phil 1:1–11
	Monday	Josh 1:1–18	Phil 1:12–26
	Tuesday	Josh 2:1–24	Phil 1:27–2:11
	Wednesday	Josh 3:1–17; 4:14–19; 5:10–12	Phil 2:12–30
	Thursday	Josh 5:13–6:21	Phil 3:1–16
	Friday	Josh 7:4–26	Phil 3:17–4:9
	Saturday	Josh 10:1–15	Phil 4:10–23
Week XI	Sunday	Josh 24:1–7, 13–28	Isa 44:12–45:3
	Monday	Judg 2:6–3:4	Ezra 1:1–8; 2:68–3:8
	Tuesday	Judg 4:1–24	Ezra 4:1–5, 24–5:5
	Wednesday	Judg 6:1–6, 11–24	Hag 1:1–2:9
	Thursday	Judg 7:1–8, 16–22a	Hag 2:10–23
	Friday	Judg 8:22–32; 9:1–15	Zech 1:1–21
	Saturday	Judg 11:1–9, 29–40	Zech 2:1–13
Week XII	Sunday	Judg 13:1–25	Zech 3:1–4:14
	Monday	Judg 16:4–6, 16–31	Zech 8:1–17, 20–23
	Tuesday	1 Sam 1:1–19	Ezra 6:1–5, 14–22
	Wednesday	1 Sam 1:20–28; 2:11–21	Ezra 7:6–28
	Thursday	1 Sam 2:22–36	Ezra 9:1–9, 15–10:5
	Friday	1 Sam 3:1–21	Neh 1:1–2:8
	Saturday	1 Sam 4:1–18	Neh 2:9–20
Week XIII	Sunday	1 Sam 5:1,6–6:4	Neh 4:1–23

		Year 1	Year 2
	Monday	1 Sam 7:15–8:22	Neh 5:1–19
	Tuesday	1 Sam 9:1–6, 14–10:1	Neh 7:73b–8:18
	Wednesday	1 Sam 11:1–15	Neh 9:1–2, 5–21
	Thursday	1 Sam 12:1–25	Neh 9:22–37
	Friday	1 Sam 15:1–23	Neh 12:27–47
	Saturday	1 Sam 16:1–13	Isa 59:1–14
Week XIV	Sunday	1 Sam 17:1–10, 23b–26, 40–51	Prov 1:1–7, 20–33
	Monday	1 Sam 17:57–18:9, 20–30	Prov 3:1–20
	Tuesday	1 Sam 19:8–10; 20:1–17	Prov 8:1–5, 12–36
	Wednesday	1 Sam 21:1–9; 22:1–5	Prov 9:1–18
	Thursday	1 Sam 25:14–24, 28–39	Prov 10:6–32
	Friday	1 Sam 26:2–25	Prov 15:8–30; 16:1–9
	Saturday	1 Sam 28:3–25	Prov 31:10–31
Week XV	Sunday	1 Sam 31:1–4; 2 Sam 1:1–16	Job 1:1–22
	Monday	2 Sam 2:1–11; 3:1–5	Job 2:1–13
	Tuesday	2 Sam 4:2–5:7	Job 3:1–26
	Wednesday	2 Sam 6:1–23	Job 4:1–21
	Thursday	2 Sam 7:1–25	Job 5:1–27
	Friday	2 Sam 11:1–17, 26–27	Job 6:1–30
	Saturday	2 Sam 12:1–25	Job 7:1–21
Week XVI	Sunday	2 Sam 15:7–14, 24–30; 16:5–13	Job 11:1–20
	Monday	2 Sam 18:6–19:4	Job 12:1–25
	Tuesday	2 Sam 24:1–25	Job 13:13–14:6
	Wednesday	1 Chr 22:5–19	Job 18:1–21
	Thursday	1 Kgs 1:11–35; 2:10–12	Job 19:1–29
	Friday	1 Kgs 3:5–28	Job 22:1–30
	Saturday	1 Kgs 8:1–21	Job 23:1–24:12
Week XVII	Sunday	1 Kgs 8:22–34, 54–61	Job 28:1–28
	Monday	1 Kgs 10:1–13	Job 29:1–10; 30:1, 9–23
	Tuesday	1 Kgs 11:1–4, 26–43	Job 31:1–23, 35–37

		Year 1	Year 2
	Wednesday	1 Kgs 12:1–19	Job 32:1–6; 33:1–22
	Thursday	1 Kgs 12:20–33	Job 38:1–30; 40:1–5
	Friday	1 Kgs 16:29–17:16	Job 40:6–24; 42:1–6
	Saturday	1 Kgs 18:16b–40	Job 42:7–17
Week XVIII	Sunday	1 Kgs 19:1–21	Obad 1–21
	Monday	1 Kgs 21:1–21, 27–29	Joel 1:13–2:11
	Tuesday	1 Kgs 22:1–9, 15–23, 29, 34–38	Joel 2:12–27
	Wednesday	2 Chr 20:1–9, 13–24	Joel 2:28–3:8
	Thursday	2 Kgs 2:1–15	Joel 3:9–21
	Friday	2 Kgs 3:5–27	Mal 1:1–14; 2:13–16
	Saturday	2 Kgs 4:8–37	Mal 3:1–4:6
Week XIX	Sunday	2 Kgs 4:38–44; 6:1–7	Jonah 1:1–17; 2:10
	Monday	2 Kgs 5:1–19a	Jonah 3:1–4:11
	Tuesday	2 Kgs 6:8–23	Zech 9:1–10:2
	Wednesday	2 Kgs 6:24–25, 32–7:16	Zech 10:3–11:3
	Thursday	2 Kgs 9:1–16, 22–27	Zech 11:4–12:8
	Friday	2 Kgs 11:1–21	Zech 12:9–13:9
	Saturday	2 Kgs 13:10–25	Zech 14:1–21
Week XX	Sunday	Eph 1:1–14	Eccles 1:1–18
	Monday	Eph 1:15–23	Eccles 2:1–26
	Tuesday	Eph 2:1–10	Eccles 3:1–22
	Wednesday	Eph 2:11–22	Eccles 5:10–6:8
	Thursday	Eph 3:1–13	Eccles 6:12–7:28
	Friday	Eph 3:14–21	Eccles 8:5–9:10
	Saturday	Eph 4:1–16	Eccles 11:7–12:14
Week XXI	Sunday	Eph 4:17–24	Tit 1:1–16
	Monday	Eph 4:25–5:7	Tit 2:1–3:2
	Tuesday	Eph 5:8–20	Tit 3:3–15
	Wednesday	Eph 5:21–33	1 Tim 1:1–20
	Thursday	Eph 6:1–9	1 Tim 2:1–15
	Friday	Eph 6:10–24	1 Tim 3:1–16
	Saturday	Philem 1–25	1 Tim 4:1–5:2
Week XXII	Sunday	2 Kgs 14:1–27	1 Tim 5:3–25
	Monday	Amos 1:1–2:3	1 Tim 6:1–10
	Tuesday	Amos 2:4–16	1 Tim 6:11–21

		Year 1	Year 2
	Wednesday	Amos 3:1–15	2 Tim 1:1–18
	Thursday	Amos 4:1–13	2 Tim 2:1–21
	Friday	Amos 5:1–17	2 Tim 2:22–3:17
	Saturday	Amos 5:18–6:14	2 Tim 4:1–22
Week XXIII	Sunday	Amos 7:1–17	2 Pet 1:1–11
	Monday	Amos 8:1–14	2 Pet 1:12–21
	Tuesday	Amos 9:1–15	2 Pet 2:1–8
	Wednesday	Hos 1:1–9; 3:1–5	2 Pet 2:9–22
	Thursday	Hos 2:2–23	2 Pet 3:1–10
	Friday	Hos 4:1–10; 5:1–7	2 Pet 3:11–18
	Saturday	Hos 5:15b–7:2	Jude 1–25
Week XXIV	Sunday	Hos 8:1–13	Esther 1:1–3, 9–16, 19; 2:5–10, 16–17
	Monday	Hos 9:1–14	Esther 3:1–11
	Tuesday	Hos 10:1–15	Esther 4:1–16
	Wednesday	Hos 11:1–11	Esther 14:1–19
	Thursday	Hos 13:1–16	Esther 5:1–14; 7:1–10
	Friday	Hos 14:1–9	Baruch 1:14–2:5; 3:1–8
	Saturday	2 Kgs 15:1–5, 32–35; 16:1–8	Baruch 3:9–15, 24–4:4
Week XXV	Sunday	Is 6:1–13	Tobit 1:1–22
	Monday	Is 3:1–15	Tobit 2:1–3:6
	Tuesday	Is 5:8–13, 17–24	Tobit 3:7–17
	Wednesday	Is 7:1–17	Tobit 4:1–5, 19–21; 5:1–16
	Thursday	Is 9:8–10:4	Tobit 6:1–17
	Friday	Is 28:1–6, 14–22	Tobit 7:1, 8b–17; 8:5–13
	Saturday	Mic 1:1–9; 2:1–11	Tobit 10:7c–11:15
Week XXVI	Sunday	Mic 3:1–12	Judith 2:1–6; 3:6; 4:1–2, 9–15
	Monday	Mic 6:1–15	Judith 5:1–21
	Tuesday	2 Kgs 17:1–18	Judith 6:1–21; 7:1, 4–5
	Wednesday	2 Kgs 17:24–41	Judith 8:1a, 10–14, 28–33; 9:1–14
	Thursday	2 Chr 29:1–2; 30:1–16a	Judith 10:1–5, 11–17; 11:1–8, 20–23
	Friday	Is 20:1–6	Judith 12:1–13:2
	Saturday	2 Kgs 20:1–19	Judith 13:3–14:7
Week XXVII	Sunday	Is 22:1–14	Sir 1:1–20
	Monday	Is 30:1–18	Sir 2:1–18
	Tuesday	2 Kgs 18:17–36	Sir 3:1–16
	Wednesday	2 Kgs 18:37–19: 19, 35–37	Sir 3:17–4:10

	Year 1	**Year 2**
Thursday	Is 37:21–35	Sir 5:1–6:4
Friday	2 Kgs 21:1–18, 23–22:1	Sir 6:5–37
Saturday	Zeph 1:1–7, 14–2:3	Sir 7:22–36

Week XXVIII

	Year 1	**Year 2**
Sunday	Zeph 3:8–20	Sir 10:6–18
Monday	Jer 1:1–19	Sir 11:11–28
Tuesday	Jer 2:1–13, 20–25	Sir 14:20–15:10
Wednesday	Jer 3:1–5, 19–4:4	Sir 15:11–20
Thursday	Jer 4:5–8, 13–28	Sir 16:24–17:14
Friday	Jer 7:1–20	Sir 17:15–32
Saturday	Jer 9:2–12, 17–22	Sir 24:1–22

Week XXIX

	Year 1	**Year 2**
Sunday	2 Kgs 22:8, 10–23:4, 21–23	Sir 26:1–4, 9–18
Monday	Nahum 1:1–8; 3:1–7, 12–15a	Sir 27:22–28, 7
Tuesday	2 Chr 35:20–36:12	Sir 29:1–13; 31:1–4
Wednesday	Hab 1:1–2:4	Sir 35:1–17
Thursday	Hab 2:5–20	Sir 38:24–39:11
Friday	Jer 22:10–30	Sir 42:15–25; 43:27–33
Saturday	Jer 19:1–5, 10–20:6	Sir 51:1–12

Week XXX

	Year 1	**Year 2**
Sunday	Jer 23:9–17, 21–29	Wisd 1:1–15
Monday	Jer 25:15–17, 27–38	Wisd 1:16–2:24
Tuesday	Jer 36:1–10, 21–32	Wis 3:1–19
Wednesday	Jer 24:1–10	Wis 4:1–20
Thursday	Jer 27:1–15	Wisd 5:1–23
Friday	Jer 28:1–17	Wid 6:1–25
Saturday	Jer 29:1–14	Wisd 7:15–30

Week XXXI

	Year 1	**Year 2**
Sunday	2 Kgs 24:20b–25:13, 18–21	Wisd 8:1–21
Monday	Jer 37:21; 38:14–28	Wisd 9:1–18
Tuesday	Jer 32:6–10, 26–40	Wisd 10:1–11:4
Wednesday	Jer 30:18–31:9	Wisd 11:20b–12:2, 11b–19
Thursday	Jer 31:15–22, 27–34	Wisd 13:1–10; 14:15–21; 15:1–6
Friday	Jer 42:1–16; 43:4–7	Wisd 15:18–16: 13, 20–25
Saturday	Ezek 1:3–14, 22–2:28	Wisd 18:1–15a; 19:4–9

		Year 1	**Year 2**
Week XXXII	Sunday	Ezek 2:8–3:11, 16–21	1 Macc 1:1–24
	Monday	Ezek 5:1–17	1 Macc 1:41–64
	Tuesday	Ezek 8:1–6a, 16–9:11	2 Macc 6:12–31
	Wednesday	Ezek 10:18–22; 11:14–25	2 Macc 7:1–19
	Thursday	Ezek 12:1–16	2 Macc 7:20–41
	Friday	Ezek 13:1–16	1 Macc 2:1, 15–28, 42–50, 65–70
	Saturday	Ezek 14:12–23	1 Macc 3:1–26
Week XXXIII	Sunday	Ezek 16:3–19, 35–43, 59–63	1 Macc 4:36–59
	Monday	Ezek 17:3–15, 19–24	2 Macc 12:36–45
	Tuesday	Ezek 18:1–13, 20–32	1 Macc 6:1–17
	Wednesday	Ezek 20:27–44	1 Macc 9:1–22
	Thursday	Ezek 24:15–27	Dan 1:1–21
	Friday	Ezek 28:1–19	Dan 2:1, 25–47
	Saturday	Ezek 34:1–6, 11–16, 25–31	Dan 3:8–23, 24–30
Week XXXIV	Sunday	Solemnity of Christ the King Dan 7:1–27	
	Monday	Ezek 36:16–36	Dan 5:1–17, 23–31
	Tuesday	Ezek 37:1–14	Dan 6:4–27
	Wednesday	Ezek 37:15–28	Dan 8:1–26
	Thursday	Ezek 38:14–39:10	Dan 9:1–4, 18–27
	Friday	Ezek 40:1–4; 43: 1–12; 44:6–9	Dan 10:1–21
	Saturday	Ezek 47:1–12	Dan 12:1–13

TABLE OF MOVABLE FEASTS

A.D.	I Sunday of Advent	Ash Wed.	Easter	Ascension	Pentecost
1972	Dec. 3	Feb. 16	Apr. 2	May 11	May 21
1973	Dec. 2	Mar. 7	Apr. 22	May 31	June 10
1974	Dec. 1	Feb. 27	Apr. 14	May 23	June 2
1975	Nov. 30	Feb. 12	Mar. 30	May 8	May 18
1976	Nov. 28	Mar. 3	Apr. 18	May 27	June 6
1977	Nov. 27	Feb. 23	Apr. 10	May 19	May 29
1978	Dec. 3	Feb. 8	Mar. 26	May 4	May 14
1979	Dec. 2	Feb. 28	Apr. 15	May 24	June 3
1980	Nov. 30	Feb. 20	Apr. 6	May 15	May 25
1981	Nov. 29	Mar. 4	Apr. 19	May 28	June 7
1982	Nov. 28	Feb. 24	Apr. 11	May 20	May 30
1983	Nov. 27	Feb. 16	Apr. 3	May 12	May 22
1984	Dec. 2	Mar. 7	Apr. 22	May 31	June 10
1985	Dec. 1	Feb. 20	Apr. 7	May 16	May 26
1986	Nov. 30	Feb. 12	Mar. 30	May 8	May 18
1987	Nov. 29	Mar. 4	Apr. 19	May 28	June 7
1988	Nov. 27	Feb. 17	Apr. 3	May 12	May 22
1989	Dec. 3	Feb. 8	Mar. 26	May 4	May 14
1990	Dec. 2	Feb. 28	Apr. 15	May 24	June 3

INDEX OF PSALMS AND CANTICLES

INDEX OF SHORT SCRIPTURE READINGS

INDEX OF HYMNS AND METRICAL PSALMS

INDEX OF HYMN TUNES: METRICAL

INDEX OF HYMN TUNES: ALPHABETICAL